William to Shakespeare.

lect his royalties, he would be among the most prosperous of playwrights.

During the eighteenth century but mostly in the nineteenth, Shakespeare's works became "immortal classics," and the cult of Shakespeare-worship was inaugurated. The plays were largely removed from their proper place on the stage into the library where they became works of literature rather than drama and were regarded as long poems, attracting all the artistic and psuedo-artistic atmosphere surrounding poetry. In the nineteenth century this attitude was friendly but later, and especially in the early twentieth century, a strange feeling arose in the English-speaking world that poetry was sissy stuff, not for men but for "pansies" and women's clubs. This of course is sheer nonsense.

This outline will present a detailed analysis of the play and background information which will show the play in its proper perspective. This means seeing the play in relation to the other plays, to the history of the times when they were written, and in relation to the theatrical technique required for their successful performance.

G. B. Harrison's book *Introducing Shakespeare*, published by Penguin Books, will be of value for general information about Shakespeare and his plays. For reference material on the Elizabethan Theater, consult E. K. Chambers, *The Elizabethan Theatre* (four volumes). For study of the organization and production methods of this theater see *Henslowe's Diary* edited by W. W. Greg. Again for general reading the student will enjoy Margaret Webster's *Shakespeare Without Tears*, published by Whittlesey House (McGraw-Hill) in 1942.

The remainder of the Introduction will be divided into sections discussing Shakespeare's life, his plays, and his theater.

LIFE OF WILLIAM SHAKESPEARE

From the standpoint of one whose main interest lies with the plays themselves, knowledge of Shakespeare's life is not very important. Inasmuch as it treats of the period between 1592 and 1611, when the plays were being written, knowledge of his life is useful in that it may give some clues as to the topical matters introduced into the plays. For instance, the scene of Hamlet's advice to the players (Act III Scene ii) takes on an added significance when considered along with the fame and bombastic style of Edward Alleyn, the then famous actor-manager of the Lord Admiral's Players (the most powerful rivals of Shakespeare's company).

This biography is pieced together from the surviving public records of the day, from contemporary references in print, and from the London Stationer's Register. It is by no means complete. The skeletal nature of the biographical material available to scholars has led commentators in the past to invent part of the story to fill it out. These parts have frequently been invented by men who were more interested in upholding a private theory than in telling the truth, and this habit of romancing has led to a tradition of inaccurate Shakespearian biography. For this reason this outline may be of use in disposing of bad traditions.

In the heyday of the self-made man, the story developed that Shakespeare was a poor boy from the village, virtually uneducated, who fled from Stratford to London to escape prosecution for poaching on the lands of Sir Thomas Lucy, and there by his talent and a commendable industry raised himself to greatness. This rags-to-riches romance was in the best Horatio Alger tradition but was emphatically not true. The town records of Stratford make it clear that John Shakespeare, father of the playwright, was far from a pauper. He was a wealthy and responsible citizen who held in turn several municipal offices. He married (1557) Mary Arden, the daughter of a distinguished Catholic family. William, their third son, was baptized in the Parish Church in 1564. He had a good grammar school education. Ben Jonson's remark that Shakespeare had "small Latin and less Greek" did not mean the same in those days, when the educated man had a fluent command of

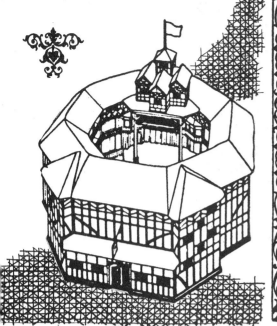

Exterior view of "The Globe"

Interior view of "The Globe"

an introduction
to Shakespeare

Latin and probably at least a reading knowledge of Greek, as it does now when classical scholars are few. The remark has been construed by the Horatio Alger people as meaning that Shakespeare reached London a semiliterate bumpkin; it is nonsense. It means merely that Shakespeare was not a university man, as most of the writers were, and that the University Wits were taking out their jealousy in snobbery and pointing out that Shakespeare used less purely literary symbolism than they did.

Shakespeare married Ann Hathaway when he was eighteen years old. She was some years older than he and the marriage seems to have been a rather hasty affair. Five months after the marriage, Suzanna, the first child, was born. Two years later, in 1585, twins Hamnet and Judith were baptized.

No one knows when Shakespeare came to London. The first mention of him occurs in the bad-tempered pamphlet which Robert Greene, one of the University Wits and a famous playwright, wrote just before his death. Greene complains of "an upstart crow, beautified with our feathers, that with his tiger's heart wrapped in a player's hide, supposes he is as well able to bombast out a blank verse as the best of you; and being an absolute Yohannes factotum, is in his own conceit the only Shakescene in a country." This was written in 1592 and indicates not only that Shakespeare was in London at the time, but that he was writing plays and beginning to make such a name for himself as to call forth the jealous apprehension of an established writer.

The next year, 1593, was a year of plague, and by order of the Lord Mayor and the Aldermen, the theaters were closed. The players, disorganized by this action, went on tour outside of London. During this year Shakespeare's two long poems, *Venus and Adonis* and *The Rape of Lucrece,* were entered in the Stationer's Register. Both were dedicated to the Earl of Southampton.

The public theaters had not been established very long. The first of these, called the Theatre, was built for James Burbage in 1576. By 1594, there were three such theaters in London, the two new houses being the Curtain and the Rose. By 1594, also, the three most celebrated of the writers, Kyd, Greene, and Marlowe were dead, and Shakespeare had already a considerable reputation. Before this date the theaters had been largely low class entertainment and the plays had been of rather poor quality. Through the revival of classical drama in the schools (comedies) and the Inns of Court (tragedies), an interest had been created in the stage. The noblemen of the time were beginning to attend the public theaters, and their tastes demanded a better class of play.

Against the background of this

Complete Study Edition

Twelfth Night

Commentary | Complete Text | Glossary

edited by
SIDNEY LAMB
Associate Professor of English,
Sir George Williams University, Montreal

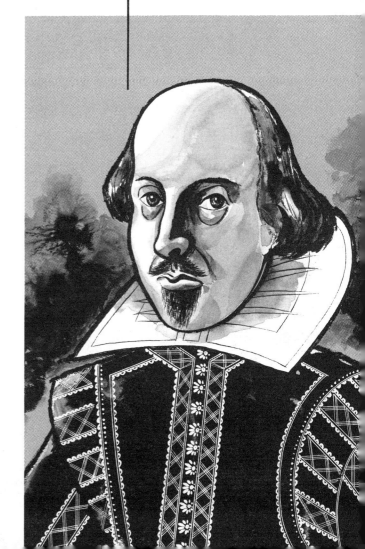

Cliff's Notes INCORPORATED

LINCOLN, NEBRASKA 68501

ISBN 0-8220-1445-9

Originally published under the title "Twelfth Night: Complete Study Guide," copyright © 1965.

Twelfth Night

SHAKESPEARE WAS NEVER MORE MEANINGFUL—

. . . than when read in Cliff's "Complete Study Edition." The introductory sections give you all of the background information about the author and his work necessary for reading with understanding and appreciation. A descriptive bibliography provides guidance in the selection of works for further study. The inviting three-column arrangement of the complete text offers the maximum in convenience to the reader. Adjacent to the text there is a running commentary that provides clear supplementary discussion of the play as it develops. Obscure words and obsolete usages used by Shakespeare are explained in the glosses directly opposite to the line in which they occur. The numerous allusions are also clarified.

SIDNEY LAMB—

. . . the editor of this Shakespeare "Complete Study Edition," attended Andover Academy and Columbia University, receiving the Prince of Wales Medal for Philosophy and the Moyes Travelling Fellowship. Following graduate studies in Elizabethan literature at King's College, Cambridge, from 1949 to 1952, he became a member of the English Faculty of the University of London's University of the Gold Coast in West Africa. Professor Lamb joined the faculty of Sir George Williams University, Montreal, in 1956.

Twelfth Night

contents

h bene fundry times publiquely :
ht Honoyrable the Lord Cham
his Seruants.

THE
MOST EX.
cellent and lamentable
Tragedie, of Romeo
and *Iuliet*.

an introduction

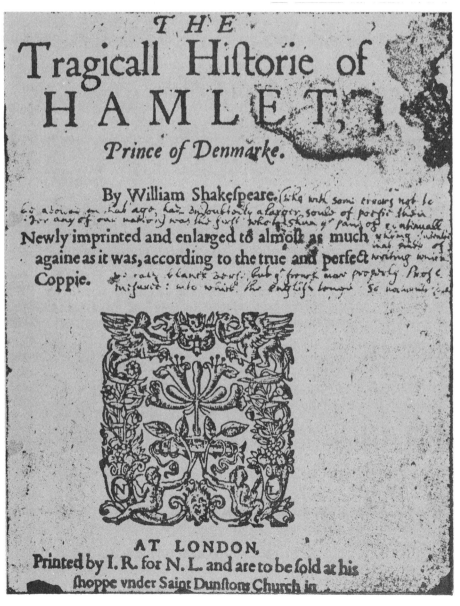

THE
Tragicall Hiftorie of
HAMLET,
Prince of Denmarke.

By William Shakefpeare.

Newly imprinted and enlarged tô almoft as much
againe as it was, according to the true and perfect
Coppie.

AT LONDON,
Printed by I. R. for N. L. and are to be fold at his
fhoppe vnder Saint Dunftons Church in

Two books are essential to the library of any English-speaking household; one of these is the Bible and the other is the works of William Shakespeare. These books form part of the house furnishings, not as reading material generally, but as the symbols of religion and culture—sort of a twentieth-century counterpart of the ancient Roman household gods. This symbolic status has done a great deal of damage both to religion and to Shakespeare.

Whatever Shakespeare may have been, he was not a deity. He was a writer of popular plays, who made a good living, bought a farm in the country, and retired at the age of about forty-five to enjoy his profits as a gentleman. The difference between Shakespeare and the other popular playwrights of his time was that he wrote better plays —plays that had such strong artistic value that they have been popular ever since. Indeed, even today, if Shakespeare could col-

increasing status and upper-class popularity of the theaters, Shakespeare's company was formed. After the 1594 productions under Alleyn, this group of actors divided. Alleyn formed a company called the Lord Admiral's Company which played in Henslowe's Rose Theatre. Under the leadership of the Burbages (James was the owner of the Theatre and his son Richard was a young tragic actor of great promise), Will Kemp (the famous comedian), and William Shakespeare, the Lord Chamberlain's Company came into being. This company continued throughout Shakespeare's career. It was renamed in 1603, shortly after Queen Elizabeth's death, becoming the King's Players.

The company played at the Theatre until Burbage's lease on the land ran out. The landlord was not willing to come to satisfactory terms. The company moved across the river and built the new Globe theater. The principal sharers in the new place were Richard and Cuthbert Burbage each with two and a half shares and William Shakespeare, John Heminge, Angustus Phillips, Thomas Pope, and Will Kemp, each with one share.

Burbage had wanted to establish a private theater and had rented the refectory of the old Blackfriars' monastery. Not being allowed to use this building he leased it to a man called Evans who obtained permission to produce plays acted by chil-dren. This venture was so successful as to make keen competition for the existing companies. This vogue of child actors is referred to in *Hamlet,* Act II Scene ii.

The children continued to play at Blackfriars until, in 1608, their license was suspended because of the seditious nature of one of their production. By this time the public attitude towards the theaters had changed, and Burbage's Company, now the King's Players, could move into the Blackfriars theater.

Partners with the Burbages in this enterprise were Shakespeare, Heminge, Condell, Sly, and Evans. This was an indoor theater, whereas the Globe had been outdoors. The stage conditions were thus radically altered. More scenery could be used; lighting effects were possible. Shakespeare's works written for this theater show the influence of change in conditions.

To return to the family affairs of the Shakespeares, records show that in 1596 John Shakespeare was granted a coat of arms and, along with his son, was entitled to call himself "gentleman." In this year also, William Shakespeare's son Hamnet died. In 1597 William Shakespeare bought from William Underwood a sizable estate at Stratford, called New Place.

Shakespeare's father died in 1601, his mother, in 1608. Both of his daughters married, one in 1607, the other in 1616.

During this time, Shakespeare went on acquiring property in Stratford. He retired to New Place probably around 1610 although this date is not definitely established, and his career as a dramatist was practically at an end. *The Tempest,* his last complete play, was written around the year 1611.

The famous will, in which he left his second best bed to his wife, was executed in 1616 and later on in that same year he was buried.

THE PLAYS

Thirty-seven plays are customarily included in the works of William Shakespeare. Scholars have been at great pains to establish the order in which these plays were written. The most important sources of information for this study are the various records of performances which exist, the printed editions which came out during Shakespeare's career, and such unmistakable references to current events as may crop up in the plays. The effect of the information gathered in this way is generally to establish two dates between which a given play must have been written. In *Hamlet* for instance, there is a scene in which Hamlet refers to the severe competition given to the adult actors by the vogue for children's performances. This vogue first became a serious threat to the professional companies in about 1600. In 1603 a very bad edition was published, without authorization, of *The*

Elizabethan types

Lute, standing cup, stoop

Queen Elizabeth

an introduction to Shakespeare

Tragical History of Hamlet, Prince of Denmark by William Shakespeare. These two facts indicate that *Hamlet* was written between the years of 1600 and 1603. This process fixed the order in which most of the plays were written. Those others of which no satisfactory record could be found were inserted in their logical place in the series according to the noticeable development of Shakespeare's style. In these various ways we have arrived at the following chronological listing of the plays.

1591   *Henry VI Part I*
        Henry VI Part II
        Henry VI Part III
        Richard III
        Titus Andronicus
        Love's Labour Lost
        The Two Gentlemen of Verona
        The Comedy of Errors
        The Taming of the Shrew

1594   *Romeo and Juliet*
        A Midsummer Night's Dream
        Richard II
        King John
        The Merchant of Venice

1597   *Henry IV Part I*
        Henry IV Part II
        Much Ado About Nothing
        Merry Wives of Windsor
        As You Like It
        Julius Caesar
        Henry V
        Troilus and Cressida

1601   *Hamlet*
        Twelfth Night
        Measure for Measure
        All's Well That Ends Well

        Othello

1606   *King Lear*
        Macbeth
        Timon of Athens
        Antony and Cleopatra
        Coriolanus

1609   *Pericles*

1611   *Cymbeline*
        The Winter's Tale
        The Tempest
        Henry VIII

At this point it is pertinent to review the tradition of dramatic form that had been established before Shakespeare began writing. Drama in England sprang at the outset from the miracle and morality plays of the medieval guilds. These dramatized Bible stories became increasingly less religious as time passed until finally they fell into disrepute. The next development was the writing of so-called *interludes*. These varied in character but often took the form of bawdy farce. As the renaissance gathered force in England, Roman drama began to be revived at the schools and the Inns of Court. Before long English writers were borrowing plots and conventions wholesale from the classic drama. The Italian model was the most fashionable and consequently was largely adopted, but many features of the old *interludes* still persisted, especially in plays written for the public theaters.

With the development among the nobility of a taste for the theater, a higher quality of work became in demand. Very few of

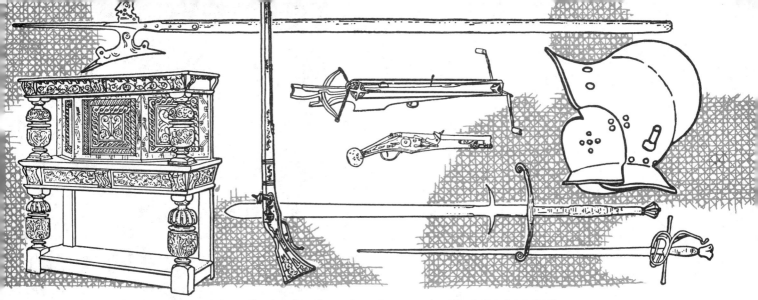

Court cupboard, crossbow, guns, sword, rapier, halberd, burgonet

the very early plays have survived. The reason for this is that the plays were not printed to be read; no one considered them worth the trouble. A play was strung together out of a set of stock characters and situations with frantic haste, often by as many as a dozen different men. These men who worked on plays did not regard their writing activity as of prime importance. They were primarily actors. With the cultivation of taste for better plays came the idea that the work of a playwright was an effort demanding special skill. The highborn audiences were interested in the plays themselves and began to include editions of their favorite plays in their libraries. With this demand for printed copies of the plays, the conception began of the dramatist as an artist in his own right, whether or not he acted himself (as most of them did).

By 1592, when Shakespeare began to make his personal reputation, a set of traditions had developed. This body of traditions gave Shakespeare the basic materials with which to work.

A special type of comedy writing had developed, centered around the name of John Lyly, designed for the sophisticated audience of the court and presented with lavish dances and decorative effects. This type of play was characterized by a delicately patterned artificiality of speech. The dialogue was studded with complicated references to Latin and Italian literature that the renaissance had made fashionable.

Shakespeare used this method extensively. In the early plays (before *The Merchant of Venice*) he was experimenting and wrote much that is nothing more than conventional. Later on, as his mature style developed, the writing becomes integral with and indispensable to the play and no longer appears artificial. In *Romeo and Juliet,* an early play, the following lines are spoken by Lady Capulet in urging Juliet to accept the Count Paris for her husband. These lines are brilliant but artificial, and the play seems to pause in order that this trick bit of word-acrobatics may be spoken.

> Read o'er the volume of young
>   Paris' face,
> And find delight, writ there
>   with beauty's pen.
> Examine every married linea-
>   ment,
> And see how one another lends
>   content:
> And what obscured in this fair
>   volume lies,
> Find written in the margent of
>   his eyes.
> This precious book of love, this
>   unbound lover,
> To beautify him only needs a
>   cover!

The other most important dramatic tradition was that of tragedy. The Elizabethan audiences liked spectacular scenes; they also had a great relish for scenes of sheer horror. This led to a school of tragic writing made popular by Kyd and Marlowe.

These plays were full of action and color and incredible wickedness, and the stage literally ran with artificial blood. Shakespeare's early tragedies are directly in this tradition, but later the convention becomes altered and improved in practice, just as that of comedy had done. The scene in *King Lear* where Gloucester has his eyes torn out stems from this convention. Lear, however, is a comparatively late play and the introduction of this scene does not distort or interrupt its organization.

Shakespeare's stylistic development falls into a quite well-defined progression. At first he wrote plays according to the habit of his rivals. He very quickly began experimenting with his technique. His main concern seems to be with tricks of language. He was finding out just what he could do. These early plays use a great deal of rhyme, seemingly just because Shakespeare liked writing rhyme. Later on, rhyme is used only when there is a quite definite dramatic purpose to justify it. Between the early plays and those which may be called mature (*The Merchant of Venice* is the first of the mature plays); there is a basic change in method. In the early works Shakespeare was taking his patterns from previous plays and writing his own pieces, quite consciously incorporating one device here and another there.

In the later period these tricks of the trade had been tested and

The world as known in 1600

Elizabethan coins

absorbed; they had become not contrived methods but part of Shakespeare's mind. This meant that, quite unconsciously, while his total attention was focused on the emotional and intellectual business of writing a masterpiece, he wrote in terms of the traditional habits he had learned and used in the earlier period. (*Henry IV, Julius Caesar, Henry V,* and *Hamlet* are the plays of this advanced stage.)

The group of plays between 1606 and 1609 shows a further new development. Having reached mastery of his medium in terms of dramatic technique (with *Othello*) and of power over the tension of thought in moving easily through scenes of comedy, pathos, and tragedy, he turned again to the actual literary quality of his plays and began to enlarge his scope quite beyond and apart from the theatrical traditions of his day. The early results of this new attempt are the two plays *King Lear* and *Macbeth*. The change in these plays is in the direction of concentration of thought. The attempt is, by using masses of images piled one on another, to convey shadings and intensities of emotion not before possible. He was trying to express the inexpressible. For example the following is from the last part of

an introduction
to Shakespeare

Lady Macbeth's famous speech in Act I, Scene v:

> Come, thick night,
> And pall thee in the dunnest smoke of hell,
> That my keen knife see not the wound it makes,
> Nor heaven peep through the blanket of the dark,
> To cry, hold, hold!

Compare the concentrated imagery of this speech with Hamlet's soliloquy at the end of Act III, Scene ii.

> 'Tis now the very witching time of night,
> When churchyards yawn, and hell itself breathes out
> Contagion to this world: now could I drink hot blood,
> And do such bitterness as the day
> Would quake to look on.

The sentiment of these two speeches is similar, but the difference in method is striking and produces a difference again in the type of effect. The *Lear-Macbeth* type of writing produces a higher tension of subtlety but tends to collect in masses rather than to move in lines as the lighter, more transparent writing of *Hamlet* does.

Shakespeare's last plays were conceived for the new indoor theater at Blackfriars and show this is in a more sophisticated type of staging. In *The Tempest,* last and most celebrated of these late comedies, there is dancing, and much complicated staging (such as the disappearing banquet, the ship at sea, and so on). The writing of plays for the

more distinguished audience of Blackfriars, and the increased stage resources there provided, influenced the form of the plays.

The writing of these plays forms a culmination. In his early apprenticeship Shakespeare had been extravagant in word-acrobatics, testing the limits of his technique. In the Lear-Macbeth period of innovation he had tried the limits of concentrated emotion to the point almost of weakening the dramatic effectiveness of the plays. In *The Tempest* his lines are shaken out into motion again. He seems to have been able to achieve the subtlety he was after in verse of light texture and easy movement, no longer showing the tendency to heaviness or opacity visible in *King Lear* and *Macbeth*.

THE THEATER

The first public theater in London was built in the year 1576 for James Burbage and was called simply The Theatre. Before this time players' companies had performed for the public in the courtyards of the city inns. For a more select public they frequently played in the great halls of institutions, notably the Inns of Court. The stage and auditorium of the Elizabethan theater were based on these traditions and combined features of both the hall and the inn-yard. The auditorium was small. There was a pit where the orchestra seats would be in a modern playhouse; this section was for the lowest classes who stood during the performances. Around the

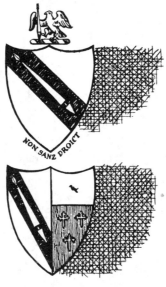

Shakespeare's Coat of Arms   Wood cut camp illustration

wall was a gallery for the gentry. The galleries and the tiring-house behind the fore-stage were roofed; the rest was open to the sky. The stage consisted of a very large platform that jutted out so that the pit audience stood on three sides of it. Behind this, under the continuation behind the stage of the gallery, was the inner stage; this was supplied with a curtain, but the open fore-stage was not. Above this inner stage was a balcony (really a continuation of the gallery), forming still another curtained stage. This gallery was used for kings addressing subjects from balconies, for the storming of walls, for Juliet's balcony and bedroom, for Cleopatra's monument and so on. Costumes and properties were extravagant (such as guillotines, fountains, ladders, etc.); extensive music was constantly used and such sound effects as cannon, drums, or unearthly screams were common; but there was no painted scenery as we know it; there was no darkness to focus attention on the stage, no facilities for stage-lighting. All these things are in marked contrast to the modern stage conventions and thus a serious problem of adaptation is posed when it comes to producing the plays under present day conditions.

The advantages are not all with the modern stage. It is true that the modern or picture stage can do more in the way of realistic effects, but this kind of realism is not important to good drama. In fact there has been a recent trend away from realistic scenery in the theater back to a conventional or stylized simplicity.

One effect of Shakespeare's stage upon his work was to make the scenes in the plays more person-scenes than place-scenes. As a matter of fact in many cases the places assigned in the texts to various scenes were not in the original and have only been added by an editor who did not understand this very fact.

It used to be said that *Antony and Cleopatra* could not be staged and was written to be read rather than acted. The grounds for this statement were that in the fourth act there were no less than fourteen scenes. To some, a scene means a change of place and requires a break in the play while scenery is shifted. To Shakespeare these scenes meant no such thing; they meant, simply, that there were fourteen different groupings of people, successively and without any break, carrying on the action of the play. The scene headings when added should have been (1) Caesar, (2) Antony and Cleopatra, (3) the common soldiers, etc., instead of (1) Before Alexandria, (2) Alexandria, a room in the palace, etc. By this you may see that with all its limitations, the Elizabethan stage had a measure of flexibility that the modern stage could envy.

Fashions in staging Shakespeare have altered radically in the last few years. At the close of the nineteenth century, Sir Herbert Beerbohm Tree staged a spectacular series of pageant productions. All the tricks of romantic realistic staging were used and, if necessary, the play was twisted, battered, and rewritten to accommodate the paraphernalia.

The modern method is to produce the plays as nearly according to the text as possible and work out a compromise to achieve the sense of space and of flexibility necessary, yet without departing so far from the stage habits of today as to confuse or divert the audience. This technique was inaugurated by Granville-Barker in the early twentieth century. With the exception of such extravagant stunts as Orson Welles' production of *Julius Caesar* in modern dress (set in Chicago and complete with tommy-guns), the prevailing practice now is to use simple, stylized scenery adapted to the needs of producing the play at full length.

Much can be done in the way of learning Shakespeare through books, but the only sure way is to see a well produced performance by a good company of actors. Whatever genius Shakespeare may have possessed as a psychologist, philosopher, or poet, he was first of all a man of the theater, who knew it from the inside, and who wrote plays so well-plotted for performance that from his day up to the present, no great actor has been able to resist them.

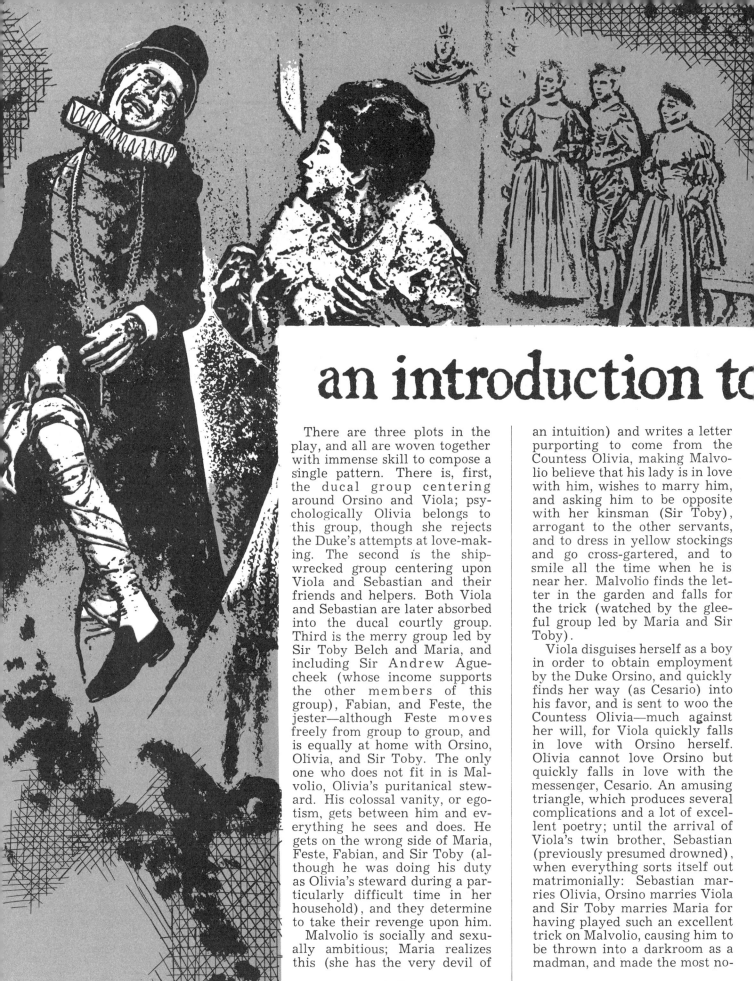

an introduction to

There are three plots in the play, and all are woven together with immense skill to compose a single pattern. There is, first, the ducal group centering around Orsino and Viola; psychologically Olivia belongs to this group, though she rejects the Duke's attempts at love-making. The second is the shipwrecked group centering upon Viola and Sebastian and their friends and helpers. Both Viola and Sebastian are later absorbed into the ducal courtly group. Third is the merry group led by Sir Toby Belch and Maria, and including Sir Andrew Aguecheek (whose income supports the other members of this group), Fabian, and Feste, the jester—although Feste moves freely from group to group, and is equally at home with Orsino, Olivia, and Sir Toby. The only one who does not fit in is Malvolio, Olivia's puritanical steward. His colossal vanity, or egotism, gets between him and everything he sees and does. He gets on the wrong side of Maria, Feste, Fabian, and Sir Toby (although he was doing his duty as Olivia's steward during a particularly difficult time in her household), and they determine to take their revenge upon him.

Malvolio is socially and sexually ambitious; Maria realizes this (she has the very devil of an intuition) and writes a letter purporting to come from the Countess Olivia, making Malvolio believe that his lady is in love with him, wishes to marry him, and asking him to be opposite with her kinsman (Sir Toby), arrogant to the other servants, and to dress in yellow stockings and go cross-gartered, and to smile all the time when he is near her. Malvolio finds the letter in the garden and falls for the trick (watched by the gleeful group led by Maria and Sir Toby).

Viola disguises herself as a boy in order to obtain employment by the Duke Orsino, and quickly finds her way (as Cesario) into his favor, and is sent to woo the Countess Olivia—much against her will, for Viola quickly falls in love with Orsino herself. Olivia cannot love Orsino but quickly falls in love with the messenger, Cesario. An amusing triangle, which produces several complications and a lot of excellent poetry; until the arrival of Viola's twin brother, Sebastian (previously presumed drowned), when everything sorts itself out matrimonially: Sebastian marries Olivia, Orsino marries Viola and Sir Toby marries Maria for having played such an excellent trick on Malvolio, causing him to be thrown into a darkroom as a madman, and made the most no-

The Comedy, Twelfth Night

torious dupe and gull that ever invention dreamed on.

This is one of the lightest, most musical, most poetic, and most delightful of Shakespeare's comedies, and ranks with *The Tempest* in its innocence and artistic caliber.

DATE OF COMPOSITION

Lord Hunsdon, the Lord Chamberlain to Queen Elizabeth I and patron of Shakespeare's company of the King's Men, was charged by the Queen with the commissioning of a play to be given at an important royal occasion in 1601. Lord Hunsdon required a play which "shalbe best furnished with rich apparell, have great variety and change of Musicke and daunces, and of a subject that may be most pleasing to her Majestie." From other evidence not connected with the royal occasion, we infer that *Twelfth Night* was written between 1599 and 1600, for performance on the sixth of January, 1601.

Dr. Leslie Hotson believes that the play was written, rehearsed and presented within a fortnight, which is not unusual with Shakespeare's plays. It seems that the play had been written at a leisurely pace, so that it might be produced on the stage with a minimum of alteration.

Twelfth Night was the Feast of the Epiphany, which fell on January 6, 1601. Actually, January 5 is the eve of Twelfth Day, or the Feast of the Epiphany, which falls twelve days after Christmas. Formerly this was a time of great merrymaking, and the games that took place were a survival of the old Roman Saturnalia, which was held in the same season. Queen Elizabeth held her elaborate entertainment at Whitehall Palace; at the magnificent ball in the evening, the comedy by Shakespeare was presented for the first time. The guest of honor was a distinguished Italian nobleman, Virginio Orsino, Duke of Bracchiano. The name Orsino in the play is a direct compliment to this nobleman. Queen Elizabeth asked him to keep his hat on during the performance, and asked him to sit next to her. He insisted on remaining standing, and the Queen chatted with him in Italian throughout the intervals.

There is little doubt from the internal and external evidence, then, that this is the correct date of composition.

The romantic plot is derived from a popular Italian comedy *Gl'Ingannati, (The Deceived)*, first performed in Sienna in 1531 by an amateur society which, amazed at its own ambition, called itself Gli Intronati, The

Thunderstruck. After passing through eight Italian editions, it was translated into French and Spanish, and into Latin by an English scholar, who called his version *Laelia*. This Latin version was performed at Queens College, Cambridge, in 1590 and again in 1598. The Shakespearean play is also indebted to a novella by Bandello. The disguise of the girl as a pageboy, the complications that ensue, the discovery at the end of the play of two *amorosos* with their *amorosas* are conventions familiar to most sixteenth-century Italian comedies.

Be the secondary sources what they may, it is certain that Shakespeare's handling of them was such as to produce a masterly and charming comedy, for which he alone should receive full credit.

THE MUSIC OF THE PLAY

In order of their occurrence, the songs and catches in this play are:
1. O mistress mine (Act II, Scene 3). Originally set to music by Thomas Morley, later by Roger Quilter and others.
2. Hold they peace, thou knave And I prithee hold thy peace (Act II, Scene 3)
3. Three merry men, and three merry men,

And three merry men be we:
I in the wood and thou on the ground,
And Jack sleeps in the tree (Act II, Scene 3)

4. There dwelt a man in Babylon
Of reputation great by fame;
He took to wife a fair woman,
Susanna she was called by name.
A woman fair and virtuous:
   Lady, lady!
Why should we not of her learn thus
   to live godly? (Act II, Scene 3)

5. Farewell dear heart refers to:
Farewell dear love, since thou wilt needs be gone,
Mine eyes do show my life is almost done.
Nay, I will never die
So long as I can spy.

....

Shall I bid her go?
What and if I do?
Shall I bid her go and spare not?
O no, no, no, no, no, I dare not. (Act II, Scene 3)

6. Come away, come away, death (Act II, Scene 4)

7. A Robin, gentle robin,
Tell me how thy leman doth,
And thou shalt know of mine.
My lady is unkind, I wis,

an introduction to the comedy, Twelfth Night

Alack, why is she so?
She loveth another better than me
And yet she will say no. (Act IV, Scene 2)

8. I am gone, sir (Act IV, Scene 2)

9. When that I was etc., (Act V, Scene 1)

The Caedmon recording of this play employs some interesting musical settings; these, however, represent only a few of the many different ones available.

CHARACTERS OF MALVOLIO, SIR TOBY BELCH, AND MARIA

Malvolio.

The nineteenth-century English essayist, Charles Lamb, or Elia, as he was affectionately known, wrote the following essay in which he stripped Malvolio of many of his ludicrous traits and presents him as an object of almost tragic interest.

"THE AUSTERE GENTLEMAN, MALVOLIO"

The part of Malvolio, in *Twelfth Night,* was performed by Bensley with a richness and dignity, of which (to judge from some recent castings of that character) the very tradition must be worn out from the stage ... Malvolio is not essentially ludicrous. He becomes comic by accident. He is cold, austere, repelling; but dignified, consistent, and, for what appears, rather of an over-stretched morality. Maria describes him as a kind of Puritan; and he might have

worn his gold chain with honour in one of our old roundhead families, in the service of a Lambert, or a Lady Fairfax. But his morality and his manners are misplaced in Illyria. He is opposed to the proper levities of the piece, and falls in the unequal contest. Still his pride, or his gravity (call it what you will), is inherent, and native to the man, not mock or affected, which latter only are the fit objects to excite laughter. His quality is at the best unlovely, but neither buffoon nor contemptible. His bearing is lofty a little above his station, but probably not much above his deserts. We see no reason why he should not have been brave, honourable, accomplished ... His careless committal of the ring to the ground (which he was commissioned to restore to Cesario), bespeaks a generosity of birth and feeling. His dialect on all occasions is that of a gentleman and a man of education. We must not confound him with the eternal old, low steward of comedy. He is the master of the household to a great princess; a dignity probably conferred upon him for other respects than age or length of service. Olivia, at the first indication of his supposed madness, declares that "she would not have him miscarry for one half of her dowry." Does this look as though this character was meant to appear little or in-

significant? Once indeed she accuses him of being—what?—"sick of self-love,"—but with a gentleness and considerateness, which could not have been, if she had not thought that this particular infirmity shaded some virtues. His rebuke to the knight, and his sottish revelers, is sensible and spirited; and when we take into consideration the unprotected condition of his mistress, and the strict regard with which her state of real or dissembled mourning would draw the eyes of the world upon her house-affairs, Malvolio might feel that the honour of the family was in some sort in his keeping; as it appears not that Olivia had any more brothers, or kinsmen, to look to it—for Sir Toby had dropped all such nice respects at the buttery-hatch. That Malvolio was meant to be represented as possessing estimable qualities, the expression of the Duke, in his anxiety to have him reconciled, almost infers: "Pursue him, and entreat him to a peace." Even in his abused state of chains and darkness, a sort of greatness seems never to desert him. He argues highly and well with the supposed Sir Topas, and philosophizes gallantly upon his straw. There must have been some shadow of worth about the man: he must have been something more than a mere vapour—a thing of straw, or Jack in of-fice—before Fabian and Maria could have ventured sending him upon a courting errand to Olivia. There was some consonancy (as he would say) in the undertaking, or the jest would have been too bold for that house of misrule.

Bensley, accordingly, threw over the part an air of Spanish loftiness. He looked, spake, and moved like an old Castilian. He was starch, spruce, opinionated, but his superstructure of pride seemed bottomed upon a sense of worth. There was something in it beyond the coxcomb. It was big and swelling, but you could not be sure that it was hollow. You might wish to see it taken down, but you felt that it was upon an elevation. He was magnificent from the outset; but when the decent sobrieties of his character began to give way, and the poison of self-love, in his conceit of the Countess's affection, gradually to work, you would have thought that the hero of La Mancha in person stood before you. How he went smiling to himself! with what ineffable carelessness would he twirl his gold chain! what a dream it was! you were infected with the illusion, and did not wish it should be removed! you had no room for laughter! if an unseasonable reflection of morality obtruded itself, it was a deep sense of the pitiable infirmity of man's nature, that can lay him open to such frenzies—but, in truth, you rather admired than pitied the lunacy while it lasted—you felt that an hour of such mistake was worth an age with the eyes open. Who would not wish to live but for a day in the conceit of such a lady's love as Olivia? Why, the Duke would have given his principality but for a quarter of a minute, sleeping or waking, to have been so deluded. The man seemed to tread upon air, to taste manna, to walk with his head in the clouds, to mate Hyperion. O! shake not the castles of his pride — endure yet for a season, bright moments of confidence—"stand still, ye watches of the element," that Malvolio may be still in fancy fair Olivia's lord! —but fate and retribution say no—I hear the mischievous titter of Maria — the witty taunts of Sir Toby—the still more insupportable triumph of the foolish knight — the counterfeit Sir Topas is unmasked—and "thus the whirligig of time," as the true clown hath it, "brings in his revenges." I confess that I never saw the catastrophe of this character, while Bensley played it, without a kind of tragic interest. There was good foolery too. Few now remember Dodd. What an Aguecheek the stage lost in him! Lovegrove, who came nearest the old actors, revived the character a few seasons

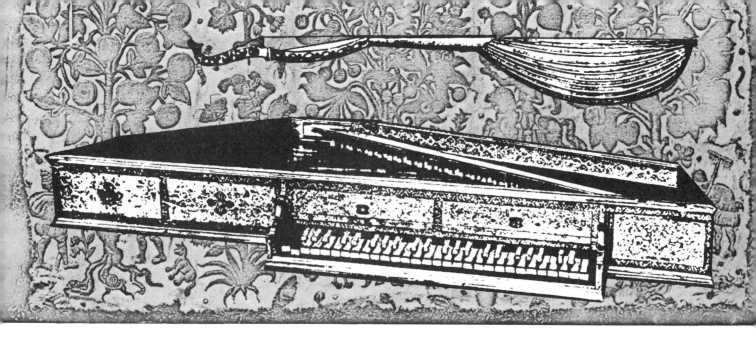

ago, and made it sufficiently grotesque; but Dodd was *it*, as it came out of nature's hands. It might be said to remain *in puribus naturalibus*. In expressing slowness of apprehension, this actor surpassed all others. You could see the first dawn of an idea stealing slowly over his countenance, climbing up by little and little, with a painful process, till it cleared up at last to the fulness of a twilight conception — its highest meridian. He seemed to keep back his intellect, as some have had the power to retard their pulsation. The balloon takes less time in filling than it took to cover the expansion of his broad moony face over all its quarters with expression. A glimmer of understanding would appear in a corner of his eye, and for lack of fuel go out again. A part of his forehead would catch a little intelligence, and be a long time in communicating it to the remainder.

Sir Toby Belch

William Hazlitt has this to say of the pair of knights, the only exclusively comic characters in the play:

They are sharply contrasted. Sir Toby, sanguine, red-nosed,

an introduction to the comedy, Twelfth Night

burly, a practical joker, always ready for "a hair of the dog that bit him," a figure after the style of Bellman; Sir Andrew, pale as though with the ague, with thin, smooth, straw-coloured hair, a wretched little nincompoop, who values himself on his dancing and fencing, quarrelsome and chicken-hearted, boastful and timid in the same breath, and grotesque in every movement. He is a mere echo and shadow of the heroes of his admiration, born to be the sport of his associates, their puppet, and their butt; and while he is so brainless as to think it possible he may win the love of the beautiful Olivia, he has at the same time an inward suspicion of his own stupidity which now and then comes in refreshingly: "Methinks sometimes I have no more wit than a Christian or an ordinary man has; but I am a great eater of beef, and, I believe, that does harm to my wit." He does not understand the simplest word he hears, and is such a mere reflex and parrot that "I too" is, as it were, the watchword of his existence. Sir Toby sums him up in the phrase: "For Andrew, if he were opened, and you find so much blood in his liver as will clog the foot of a flea, I'll eat the rest of the anatomy."

Maria

Hazlitt writes: "We have a sneaking kindness for Maria and

her rogueries . . . but does not give a full-length treatment of her." She fits in with Sir Toby Belch's view of the world, and it is true that this "youngest wren of nine" and "as pretty a piece of Eve's flesh as any in Illyria" later married him. They are both opposed to Malvolio, because they represent the "cakes and ale" of which, because he was a virtuous Puritan, Malvolio so disapproved.

THE DISGUISE THEME

The idea of disguising oneself, if female, as a pageboy to obtain masculine employment was not invented by Shakespeare, for it was a fairly common feature of Italian comedy in the sixteenth-century, and goes back to Plautus. In *Twelfth Night*, however, Shakespeare exploits the theme of disguise in several original ways, although the basic disguise situation centering on the Viola-Cesario dichotomy is conventional. In the second scene of Act I, Viola declares:

be my aid
For such disguise as haply shall become
The form of my intent.

As a beautiful young woman she would need to protect herself in order to enter (and remain in) the service of a bachelor well-known for his selfishness and sensuality.

In the second scene of Act II, however, Viola has doubts about the virtue of disguise when she says:

Disguise, I see, thou art a wickedness
Wherein the pregnant enemy does much.
How easy is it for the proper-false
In women's waxen hearts to set their forms.

In Viola's case there are sound, empirical reasons for retaining the disguise even though its retention causes injury to Olivia's emotions, since the harm that would result to Viola from shedding the disguise prematurely would be so much greater than the injury to Olivia.

The intention and effect of Maria and Toby's trick on Malvolio caused him to disguise his own identity in real life from himself, so that by his smiling and his use of opposition, arroance, yellow stockings, and cross-gartering, he believed himself to be other than he was. This is a much more insidious, subtle, and dangerous kind of disguise, since it is internal and subjective rather than external and superficial. This kind of disguise is of the order of an hallucination, or self-deception; it differs in kind as well as in degree from the objective disguise of a Viola.

Feste assumes objective, physical disguise (beard, gown, voice, intonation, pseudo-ecclesiastical vocabulary, quasi-metaphysical argumentation, etc.,) when he goes, in the guise of Sir Topas the Curate, to visit Malvolio the presumed lunatic.

The whole theme of disguise and subsequent equivocation arises in the conversation between Olivia and Viola (as Cesario) in the third Act, Scene 1.

Olivia
Stay.
I prithee tell me what thou think'st of me.

Viola
That you do think you are not what you are.

Olivia
If I think so, I think the same of you.

Viola
Then think you right: I am not what I am.

Olivia
I would you were as I would have you be.

Viola
Would it be better, madam, than I am?
I wish it might, for now I am your fool.

Olivia
O, what a deal of scorn looks beautiful
In the contempt and anger of his lip.
A murderous guilt shows not itself more soon
Than love that would seem hid. Love's night is noon;
Cesario, by the roses of the spring,
By maidhood, honour, truth and everything,
I love thee so that, maugre all thy pride,
Nor wit nor reason can my passion hide . . .

The two women fence neatly with their respective disguises, and Viola sees that although Olivia is in love with this supposed boy, nevertheless it would be fatal to disillusion her at this time since this would lead to loss of employment and probable disgrace. Besides, Shakespeare was not anxious to shed a disguise that undoubtedly brought erotic undertones and overtones to the master-mistress relationship in the scenes between Orsino and Viola (as Cesario) especially from the point of view of the single sex theater where female parts had to be sustained by boys whose voices were falsely high or not yet broken.

The shattering of the disguise of Viola after the identification beyond doubt of Sebastian is the *piece de resistance* of this disguise theme. The shedding of the disguise removes the matrimonial obstacle, and the couples realign in an acceptable way. It is the masterly building-up of the reality of the disguise that enables Shakespeare to achieve the element of surprise in the ending scene.

Dramatis Personae

ORSINO, Duke of Illyria, also called the Count
SEBASTIAN, brother to Viola
ANTONIO, a sea captain, friend to Sebastian
A Sea Captain, friend to Viola
VALENTINE }
CURIO } gentlemen attending on the Duke
SIR TOBY BELCH, uncle to Olivia
SIR ANDREW AGUECHEEK
MALVOLIO, steward to Olivia
FABIAN }
FESTE, a clown } servants to Olivia
OLIVIA, a rich Countess
VIOLA, sister to Sebastian; when disguised appears as Cesario
MARIA, Olivia's waiting-woman
Lords, Priests, Sailors, Officers, Musicians, and Attendants

SCENE: *A city in Illyria, and the sea-coast near it*

TWELFTH NIGHT

ACT I SCENE I

The play opens to the sound of music, and music (instrumental music and the music of verse) accompanies it throughout. A trio of violin, lute, and flute is on the stage, playing something sweet, languid, melancholy, and courtly to match the mood and the personality of the Duke, Orsino, who is reclining at length upon a divan for all the world like an oriental despot: there is something Turkish in Orsino's character.

Orsino is in love, not so much with a lady (the Countess Olivia has been deaf to his protestations) as with the state of love itself. A sublimely selfish gentleman, he gives himself up to the exquisite delights of his own passion and does little to reach beyond himself to the object of his (supposed) affections.

His pleasure in the instrumentalists quickly evaporates, however, in line 7, and he sends them away with an aristocratic gesture of his hand. Bowing deeply (for he is a duke), they retire. Orsino expatiates on the capacity of love, which resembles that of the sea. He is in a confused state of mind—like "fancy" invoked in line 14; "so full of shapes . . . That it alone is high fantastical." Curio recognizes this mood and tries to distract his master by mentioning hunting. Orsino wishes to go hunting the Countess Olivia, but he plays along with Curio in order to make the pun that soon follows.

The poetry in Orsino's opening speech is vowel music, open, rich, and rounded out like a riding cape in a breeze. It is affected and almost insincere—but then, so is Orsino. Notice how well Shakespeare knew how to make the manner of speech express the character.

When Curio mentions hunting the hart (male deer, or stag), Orsino immediately thinks of another kind of heart (his sweetheart), and launches into a poetic description of her qualities; he himself has become a hart (deer) and is pursued with the cruel hounds of desire.

Orsino's messenger, Valentine, now returns from visiting the Countess Olivia. She has refused him admittance, but from her serving-maid he received the answer: she is in mourning for seven years for the death of her brother. She will live cloistered like a nun. This news does not deter the Duke. If this is how she loves her dead brother, how much more will she love when she falls in love with a nobleman like me, he says. He lies down on his ottoman and dreams of sweet beds of flowers, for he believes that love thoughts lie rich when canopied with bowers.

ACT ONE, scene one.

(A ROOM IN THE DUKE'S PALACE.)

Enter DUKE, CURIO, *and other Lords;*
Musicians attending.

Duke. If music be the food of love, play on;
Give me excess of it, that, surfeiting,   2
The appetite may sicken, and so die.
That strain again! it had a dying fall.
O, it came o'er my ear like the sweet south   5
That breathes upon a bank of violets,
Stealing and giving odour! Enough; no more.
'Tis not so sweet now as it was before.
O spirit of love! how quick and fresh art thou!   9
That, nothwithstanding thy capacity
Receiveth as the sea, nought enters there,
Of what validity and pitch soe'er,   12
But falls into abatement and low price,   13
Even in a minute: so full of shapes is fancy,   14
That it alone is high fantastical.
Curio. Will you go hunt, my lord?
Duke.   What, Curio?
Curio. The hart.   18
Duke. Why, so I do, the noblest that I have.   19
O, when mine eyes did see Olivia first,
Methought she purged the air of pestilence!   21
That instant was I turn'd into a hart;   22
And my desires, like fell and cruel hounds,   23
E'er since pursue me.

Enter VALENTINE

How now! what news from her?
Valentine. So please my lord, I might not be admitted;
But from her handmaid do return this answer: 26
The element itself, till seven years' heat,   27
Shall not behold her face at ample view;
But, like a cloistress, she will veiled walk   29
And water once a day her chamber round   30
With eye-offending brine: all this to season   31
A brother's dead love, which she would keep fresh
And lasting in her sad remembrance.
Duke. O, she that hath a heart of that fine frame   34
To pay, this debt of love but to a brother,
How will she love, when the rich golden shaft   36
Hath kill'd the flock of all affections else
That live in her; when liver, brain, and heart,   38
These sovereign thrones, are all supplied, and fill'd
Her sweet perfections with one self king!   40
Away before me to sweet beds of flowers;
Love-thoughts lie rich when canopied with bowers.   42
                                            [*Exeunt.*

---

2. "surfeiting": having more than enough.

5. "south": wind (this makes much more sense than the word sound which has mistakenly crept into many other editions) Pope's emendation.

9. "O . . .": an apostrophe to the spirit of love, spoken more to himself than to his attendants (as is usual with Orsino).

12. "pitch": height.

13. "abatement": falling of powers.

14. "fancy": imagination.

18. "hart": male deer or stag.
Notice the deliberate rhetorical effects employed in Orsino's opening speech. The alliteration of the sibilant-s sounds in lines 2 and 3 is noteworthy; the assonance (play on vowel-sounds) in lines 1-15 is also remarkable. The effect is heavy and oriental in its muffled sensuality.

19. "noblest": the word hart (or perhaps heart) is understood to follow, to make clear the transition from hunting deer to Olivia.

21. "pestilence": infection (she purified the air).
In line 22 following there is an implied and slightly oblique reference to the myth of Acteon, who was turned into a hart by the goddess Diana, and who could not escape from being torn to pieces by his own hounds. This was his punishment for having accidentally viewed Diana and her nymphs while they were bathing.

23. "desires, like . . . hounds": an apt simile to describe the urgency and tracking qualities of his feelings for the lady.

26. "handmaid": personal maidservant.

27. "element": sky.

29. "cloistress": nun.

30. "chamber": room (Fr. la chambre).

31. "brine": salt tears.
"season": spice or make more acceptable.

34. "frame": quality or texture.

36. "shaft": love arrow (of Cupid).

38. "liver, brain, and heart": the liver vied with the heart as the seat of the bodily passions in the Elizabethan physiology; the brain was to control the exercise of both the affections and the passions.

40. "one self king": himself (as husband or lover).

42. "bowers": glades.

TWELFTH NIGHT

ACT I SCENE I

From this scene we gather that the Duke is a wealthy and amorous gentleman pining away for the love of the Countess Olivia who will have nothing to do with him because she is in mourning for her brother's death. We glimpse the character of Olivia, and sense that she will prove to be more interesting and sensitive than the Duke, whose selfish aestheticism somewhat repels us.

The verse is of a very high order, and the opening speech might well be memorized.

ACT I SCENE II

The scene shifts to the sea-coast of Illyria, an imaginary country ruled by the Duke Orsino. On stage this scene is usually played before the curtain to speed up the production.

We meet a girl (Viola), a sea-captain, and several sailors. They are the survivors of a shipwreck, and they assume that they are the sole survivors. In this assumption they are mistaken, but they do not realize this until the fifth act. This mistaken assumption leads to some very humorous situations of mistaken identity later in the play.

Viola's brother is presumed to be among the drowned. The captain holds out a hope that he managed to save himself, and Viola gives him some money as a reward for his optimism. She has evidently managed to hang onto her purse. Viola speaks with a seriousness and demure maidenliness which are very attractive. She has never been in this part of the world before, but the sea-captain knows the country well and tells her that Duke Orsino rules here. She has heard about Orsino from her father, and wonders if the Duke is still a bachelor. The captain believes he is, though gossip has it that he is in love with the Countess Olivia. Olivia's father died twelve months or so ago, and her brother soon followed him, so that she has been left alone with her household. For their dear love she has sworn to give up the company and even the sight of men.

Viola at once wishes to serve this lady, because she herself is in mourning for her brother Sebastian, and feels that Olivia's grief would be a fair counterpart to her own. The captain says this might be difficult to arrange.

The captain knows that Olivia will admit nobody for fear of being taken advantage of, even by

---

Scene two.

(THE SEA-COAST.)

Enter VIOLA, *a Captain, and Sailors.*

Viola. What country, friends, is this?

Captain. This is Illyria, lady. 2

Viola. And what should I do in Illyria?
My brother he is in Elysium. 4
Perchance he is not drown'd. What think you, 5
   sailors?

Captain. It is perchance that you yourself were saved. 6

Viola. Oh, my poor brother! and so perchance may
   he be.

Captain. True, madam; and, to comfort you with
   chance,
Assure yourself, after our ship did split,
When you and those poor number saved with you
Hung on our driving boat, I saw your brother,
Most provident in peril, bind himself,
Courage and hope both teaching him the practice,
To a strong mast that lived upon the sea;
Where, like Arion on the dolphin's back, 15
I saw him hold acquaintance with the waves
So long as I could see.

Viola. For saying so, there's gold.
Mine own escape unfoldeth to my hope, 19
Where to thy speech serves for authority, 20
The like of him. Know'st thou this country?

Captain. Ay, madam, well; for I was bred and born
Not three hours' travel from this very place.

Viola. Who governs here?

Captain. A noble Duke, in nature as in name. 25

Viola. What is his name?

Captain. Orsino.

Viola. Orsino! I have heard my father name him.
He was a bachelor then.

Captain. And so is now, or was so very late;
For but a month ago I went from hence,
And then 'twas fresh in murmur,—as, you know, 32
What great ones do the less will prattle of,— 33
That he did seek the love of fair Olivia.

Viola. What's she?

Captain. A virtuous maid, the daughter of a count
That died some twelvemonths since; then leaving
   her
In the protection of his son, her brother,
Who shortly also died: for whose dear love,
They say, she hath abjured the company 40
And sight of men.

Viola.   O that I served that lady,
And might not be deliver'd to the world,
Till I had made mine own occasion mellow, 43
What my estate is!

Captain.   That were hard to compass, 44
Because she will admit no kind of suit, 45
No, not the duke's.

Viola. There is a fair behaviour in thee, captain;

---

2. "Illyria": a mythical land somewhere in the Mediterranean.

4. "Elysium": paradise (the name has been suggested by Illyria).

5. "Perchance": perhaps.

6. "perchance": by chance.

15. "Arion on the dolphin's back": Arion was the poet-musician of the Greek island of Lesbos; about to be put to death by pirates, he asked for a last chance to play his lyre, then leaped overboard and was carried ashore by a dolphin that had been enchanted by the music.

19. "unfoldeth to my hope": gives support to the hope.

20. "thy speech serves for authority": your account lends additional force.

25. "nature": character.

32. "murmur": rumor, gossip.

33. "prattle": chatter.

40. "abjured": solemnly sworn to give up, sacrifice.

43. "made mine own occasion mellow": until the time was ripe for revealing my state.

44. "to compass": to bring about.

45. "suit": wooing.

18

TWELFTH NIGHT

ACT I SCENE II

the Duke and his messengers. But he has not reckoned with the determination and ingenuity of Viola.

Viola decides to trust the captain, and takes him into her confidence. She wishes to disguise herself as a young man, and thus enter into the employment of the Duke. The captain will present her as an eunuch to him, and she will be able to entertain the Duke by playing several instruments and singing to him. The only condition is that the captain shall not reveal that Viola is a girl.

The captain agrees to be her mute, and promises not to tell the secret. He leads her on.

ACT I SCENE III

We meet a third group of persons at Olivia's house. They are dissolute gentlemen and some of Olivia's servants, and they spend their time drinking, cavorting, and merry-making in the kitchens of the Countess. She is too withdrawn and ladylike to notice their misbehavior most of the time, but when she does, is disapproving. She relies on her steward, Malvolio, to keep her household in order, and this the puritanical and pedantic steward attempts (not very successfully) to do.

Sir Toby Belch, Olivia's uncle, is condemning his niece for taking her brother's death so badly. He is sure care (anxiety and grief) is an enemy of life. He is himself rather too free of cares of any kind.

Maria, Olivia's vivacious, intelligent, and mischievous kitchen-maid, tells Sir Toby that Olivia takes great exception to the hours he keeps. She warns him to discipline himself better, else Olivia may have him thrown out of her house. Olivia also disapproves of Sir Toby's friend, a foolish knight called Sir Andrew Aguecheek. This man, though foolish, has an income of three thousand ducats a year, and Toby is anxious to remain on good terms with him, though he despises him. Toby is an incipient Falstaff; Aguecheek has no parallel in literature—he is the essence of comical stupidity.

Maria is not really anxious to reform Sir Toby, nor is she a shrewish woman; but she is anxious to keep him out of trouble with his cousin, the countess Olivia. Actually, Maria is very fond of Sir Toby for at the end of the play does he not marry her?

And though that nature with a beauteous wall
Doth oft close in pollution, yet of thee   49
I will believe thou hast a mind that suits
With this thy fair and outward character.
I prithee, and I'll pay thee bounteously,
Conceal me what I am, and be my aid
For such disguise as haply shall become   54
The form of my intent. I'll serve this Duke;
Thou shalt present me as an eunuch to him.   56
It may be worth thy pains; for I can sing
And speak to him in many sorts of music,
That will allow me very worth his service.   59
What else may hap to time I will commit;   60
Only shape thou thy silence to my wit.

Captain. Be you his eunuch, and your mute I'll be.   62
When my tongue blabs, then let mine eyes not see.

Viola. I thank thee; lead me on.   [*Exeunt.*

Scene three.

(A Room in Olivia's House.)

Enter SIR TOBY BELCH *and* MARIA.

Sir Toby. What a plague means my niece, to take   1
the death of her brother thus? I am sure care's an
enemy to life.

Maria. By my troth, Sir Toby, you must come in
earlier o' nights. Your cousin, my lady, takes great   5
exceptions to your ill hours.

Sir Toby. Why, let her except, before excepted.   6

Maria. Ay, but you must confine yourself within
the modest limits of order.

Sir Toby. Confine! I'll confine myself no finer   9
than I am. These clothes are good enough to drink
in; and so be these boots too. An they be not, let
them hang themselves in their own straps.

Maria. That quaffing and drinking will undo you.
I heard my lady talk of it yesterday; and of a foolish
knight that you brought in one night here to be her
wooer.

Sir Toby. Who, Sir Andrew Aguecheek?

Maria. Ay, he.

Sir Toby. He's as tall a man as any's in Illyria.

Maria. What's that to the purpose?

Sir Toby. Why, he has three thousand ducats a year.   20

Maria. Ay, but he'll have but a year in all these
ducats; he's a very fool and a prodigal.   22

Sir Toby. Fie, that you'll say so! He plays o' the
viol-de-gamboys, and speaks three or four lan-   24
guages word for word without book, and hath all the
good gifts of nature.

Maria. He hath indeed, almost natural: for besides
that he's a fool, he's a great quarreller; and but that
he hath the gift of a coward to allay the gust he hath   28
in quarrelling, 'tis thought among the prudent he
would quickly have the gift of a grave.   30

Sir Toby. By this hand, they are scoundrels and
substractors that say so of him. Who are they?   32

---

49. "close in pollution": nature often encloses things nasty or evil in a beautiful exterior.

54. "disguise": Viola is a young lady of good birth; she would have difficulty obtaining a suitable position at Orsino's court owing to the fact that the Duke was a bachelor.

56. "eunuch": boy with a high voice (counter-tenor, male alto, or even castrato).

59. "very worth": worthy of.

60. "hap": happen.

62. "mute": slave whose tongue has been removed for security reasons, or silent person.
Taken in conjuction with eunuch, a pun is intended, because both eunuchs and mutes were associated with oriental courts.

1. "What a plague": Sir Toby frequently employs oaths in his conversation.

5. "ill hours": coming in at all hours, especially late at night or early in the morning.

6. "except": make an exception of (active) before being made an exception of (passive).

9. "Confine . . . finer": a play on words.

20. "ducats": Spanish coin worth about 6/8d then.

22. "prodigal": wastrel.

24. "viol-de-gamboys": (Italian gamba, leg) a stringed instrument like a violincello, held between the knees and scraped with a bow.

28. "gust": appetite or gusto (taste for).

30. "gift of a grave": present of death.

32. "substractors": Sir Toby cannot say subtractors after all the drink he has taken. He means detractors, those who take away a man's reputation by gossiping about him behind his back.

TWELFTH NIGHT

ACT I SCENE III

Aguecheek is both foolish and extravagant, and Sir Toby and the others take full advantage of these weaknesses. He is also a great quarreller but never follows up a quarrel to its logical conclusion, a duel, because he is such a coward. He spends most of his evenings drinking in Sir Toby's company, and you may guess who pays for the drink: not Sir Toby.

He enters now, and Sir Toby rudely calls him Sir Andrew Agueface which means Face-ache. He is tall and thin, and wears a flowing yellow wig which enhances his comic features and makes him look even more fantastical.

Toby and Andrew greet one another ecstatically, which is absurd since they meet so frequently, and Andrew acknowledges Maria in a modest manner because he is afraid of women. Sir Toby tells him to get in closer and kiss her, but Andrew does not understand the meaning of the word used to convey this.

A humorous conversation now follows between Sir Toby and Sir Andrew, in which Sir Toby is always one up over his dull-witted friend.

It appears that Toby has promised that his niece, the Countess Olivia, will show an amorous interest in Sir Andrew if he stays around a little longer. On this pretext Sir Andrew has remained, but is discouraged when he finds that Olivia is not interested in him one little bit. He knows that "the Count himself here hard by woos her" (he mistakes the Duke's title) and threatens to go home.

Maria. They that add, moreover, he's drunk nightly in your company.

Sir Toby. With drinking healths to my niece. I'll drink to her as long as there is a passage in my throat and drink in Illyria. He's a coward and a coystrill that will not drink to my niece till his brains turn o' the toe like a parish-top. What, wench! Castiliano vulgo! for here comes sir Andrew Agueface. 37
39

Enter SIR ANDREW AGUECHEEK

Sir Andrew. Sir Toby Belch! how now, Sir Toby Belch!

Sir Toby. Sweet Sir Andrew!

Sir Andrew. Bless you, fair shrew.

Maria. And you too, sir.

Sir Toby. Accost, Sir Andrew, accost. 45

Sir Andrew. What's that?

Sir Toby. My Niece's chamber-maid.

Sir Andrew. Good Mistress Accost, I desire better 48
acquaintance.

Maria. My name is Mary, sir.

Sir Andrew. Good Mistress Mary Accost,—

Sir Toby. You mistake, knight: accost is, front her, board her, woo her, assail her.

Sir Andrew. By my troth, I would not undertake her 53
in this company. Is that the meaning of accost?

Maria. Fare you well gentlemen.

Sir Toby. An thou let part so, Sir Andrew, would thou mightst never draw sword again.

Sir Andrew. An you part so, mistress, I would I might never draw sword again. Fair lady, do you think you have fools in hand?

Maria. Sir, I have not you by the hand.

Sir Andrew. Marry, but you shall have; and here's my hand.

Maria. Now, sir, thought is free. I pray you, bring your hand to the butter-bar and let it drink. 64

Sir Andrew. Wherefore, sweetheart? what's your metaphor?

Maria. It's dry, sir.

Sir Andrew. Why, I think so; I am not such an ass but I can keep my hand dry. But what's your jest?

Maria. A dry jest, sir.

Sir Andrew. Are you full of them?

Maria. Ay, sir; I have them at my fingers' ends: marry, now I let go your hand I am barren.

                  [*Exit* MARIA.

Sir Toby. O knight, thou lackest a cup of canary. 73
When did I see thee so put down?

Sir Andrew. Never in your life, I think, unless you see canary put me down. Methinks sometimes I have no more wit than a Christian or an ordinary man has; but I am a great eater of beef, and I believe that does harm to my wit.

Sir Toby. No question.

Sir Andrew. An I thought that, I'd forswear it. I'll 80
ride home to-morrow, Sir Toby.

Sir Toby. Pourquoi, my dear knight? 82

Sir Andrew. What is "pourquoi"? do or not do? I would I had bestowed that time in the tongues that I have in fencing, dancing, and bear-baiting. O, had

37. "coystrill": knave or base fellow.

39. "Castiliano vulgo": either put on the grave manner of the Castilian aristocrat, for here comes the 'knight of the sorrowful countenance' Sir Andrew Agueface, or think of the common 'castilians' (coins worth 5/-. Andrew supplied Toby with money.

45. "accost": speak to first, come up to and address.

48. "Accost": to make up to or to woo.

53. "troth": in truth.

64. "butter-bar": a room or pantry in which the wines and liquors are kept.

73. "canary": light sweet wine from the Canary Islands.

80. "forswear it": swear to give it up.

82. "Pourquoi": Fr. for why.

TWELFTH NIGHT

ACT I SCENE III

Toby assures him that she will have nothing to do with the count, and Andrew rashly promises to stay a month longer. They drink and prepare to indulge in some revels —undertaken usually at Andrew's expense.

The characters of both Sir Toby and Sir Andrew are revealed here. Sir Toby takes the initiative, and Sir Andrew follows—except when it came to paying bills, in which case Toby relied upon Andrew's three thousand ducats a year.

Sir Toby asks Andrew if he is good at these "kickshawses" (revels) and Andrew says that he is in such a manner that it is evident he is not.

They joke about dancing and cutting a caper, and determine to do some jumping and gallivanting around. They go out leaping higher and higher, and shouting and laughing at the tops of their voices. A noisy, unruly, comic crew!

ACT I SCENE IV

At the Duke Orsino's palace, we meet Viola again. She has successfully carried out her plan, and disguised as a boy, Cesario, has been taken on as a member of the ducal household. Orsino has taken a fancy to Cesario, and is employing him as a personal messenger, or proxy, to go to the Countess Olivia's house bearing messages of love. Valentine, the captain, knows Cesario's real identity and tells

---

I but followed the arts!

Sir Toby. Then hadst thou had an excellent head of hair.   86

Sir Andrew. Why, would that have mended my hair?

Sir Toby. Past question, for thou seest it will not curl by nature.

Sir Andrew. But it becomes me well enough, does't not?

Sir Toby. Excellent; it hangs like flax on a distaff.

Sir Andrew. Faith, I'll home to-morrow, Sir Toby. Your niece will not be seen; or if she be, it's four to one she'll none of me. The count himself here hard by woos her.

Sir Toby. She'll none o' the count. She'll not match above her degree, neither in estate, years, nor wit. 98 I have heard her swear't. Tut, there's life in't, man.

Sir Andrew. I'll stay a month longer. I am a fellow o' the strangest mind i' the world; I delight in masques 101 and revels sometimes altogether.

Sir Toby. Art thou good at these kickshawses, 103 knight?

Sir Andrew. As any man in Illyria, whatsoever he be, under the degree of my betters; and yet I will not compare with an old man.

Sir Toby. What is thy excellence in a galliard, 106 knight?

Sir Andrew. Faith, I can cut a caper.   108

Sir Toby. And I can cut the mutton to't.   109

Sir Andrew. And I think I have the back-trick 110 simply as strong as any man in Illyria.

Sir Toby. Wherefore are these things hid? wherefore have these gifts a curtain before 'em? are they like to take dust, like Mistress Mall's picture? why 114 dost thou not go to church in a galliard and come home in a coranto? My very walk should be a jig. What 116 dost thou mean? Is it a world to hide virtues in? I did think, by the excellent constitution of thy leg, it was formed under a star of a galliard.   120

Sir Andrew. Ay, 'tis strong, and it does indifferent well in a flame-coloured stock. Shall we set about 122 some revels?

Sir Toby. What shall we do else? were we not born under Taurus?   125

Sir Andrew. Taurus! That's sides and heart.

Sir Toby. No, sir; it is legs and thighs. Let me see thee caper. Ha! higher; ha, ha! excellent!

        [Exeunt.

Scene four.

(THE DUKE'S PALACE.)

Enter VALENTINE, *and* VIOLA *in man's attire.*

Valentine. If the duke continue these favours 1 towards you Cesario, you are like to be much advanced. He hath known you but three days, and already you are no stranger.   4

21

---

86. "hair": Sir Andrew was probably bald under the large wig he affected.

98. "degree": rank.

101. "masques": dramatic entertainments set to music.

103. "kickshawses": fancy dishes (revels, here).

106. "galliard": quick and lively dance in triple time.

108. "cut a caper": leap about.

109. "mutton": to accompany caper sauce (pun).

110. "back-trick": a difficult acrobatic leap.

114. "Mistress Mall's picture": perhaps a reference to Mistress Mary, or Mall, Fitton, one of Queen Elizabeth's maids-of-honor who had fallen from royal favor.

116. "coranto": dance with a running step.
"jig": lively dance often in triple time.

120. "formed under a star...": reference to the belief that the stars determine our destiny (astrological).

122. "stock": stocking.

125. "Taurus": the Bull; second of the twelve signs of the zodiac. Andrew confuses Taurus with Leo, as Toby points out.

1. "these favours": confiding in Cesario and sending him on confidential missions to Olivia.

2. "advanced": promoted in the ducal service.

4. "no stranger": understatement (a figure of speech know as litotes) for one of his confidential friends.

TWELFTH NIGHT

ACT I SCENE IV

him (as we shall call her from now on) that he is likely to be promoted now that Orsino has taken such a liking to him.

Orsino enters, sends everybody except Cesario away, and tells Cesario to go once more to Olivia to plead his love with her. Cesario says that if Olivia is as abandoned to her sorrow as it is rumored she is, she never will admit him. Orsino says, do not take no for an answer; overleap the limits of civility, if necessary, and get inside the house to deliver this message rather than return empty-handed. Cesario reluctantly accepts this order. But what is she to say when she does gain admittance?

Then, says Orsino, you must unfold the passion of my love; make her feel the urgency of my desire. A young man like you will be able to persuade her better than an older and more serious messenger. Cesario disagrees with this, but the Duke makes a speech praising his physical appearance, which Olivia cannot fail to respond to positively.

Orsino says that if Cesario prospers well in this, he will be well rewarded by his master.

Cesario is most reluctant to woo Olivia on Orsino's behalf for a very natural thing has taken place: Viola (Cesario) has fallen in love with Orsino herself. "Whoe'er I woo, myself would be his wife." She cannot reveal her own love, however, for fear of uncovering the disguise. This is the beginning of the love complication in this play. It will give rise to some of the loveliest poetry in the play, and, indeed, in the whole of Shakespeare.

ACT I SCENE V

In the kitchens at Olivia's house, Maria and the Clown are engaged in a verbal sparring match.
The two are well matched. Maria is a mischievous, quick-witted Cockney, and the Clown has a mind like quicksilver.

The pattern of this verbal humor carries it forward in a rapid give and take of repartee which is extremely effective on stage, and when understood by the audience is very amusing.

Viola. You either fear his humour or my negligence, that you call in question the continuance of his love. Is he inconstant, sir, in his favours? 4 6
Valentine. No, believe me.
Viola. I thank you. Here comes the count.

Enter DUKE, CURIO, *and Attendants.*

Duke. Who saw Cesario, ho?
Viola. On your attendance, my lord; here.
Duke. Stand you a while aloof. Cesario, 11
Thou know'st no less but all. I have unclasp'd 12
To thee the book even of my secret soul; 13
Therefore, good youth, address thy gait unto her; 14
Be not denied access, stand at her doors, 15
And tell them, there thy fixed foot shall grow
Till thou have audience.
Viola.   Sure, my noble lord,
If she be so abandon'd to her sorrow
As it is spoke, she never will admit me.
Duke. Be clamorous and leap all civil bounds 20
Rather than make unprofited return. 21
Viola. Say I do speak with her, my lord, what then?
Duke. Oh, then unfold the passion of my love, 23
Surprise her with discourse of my dear faith 24
It shall become thee well to act my woes;
She will attend it better in thy youth
Than in a nuncio's of more grave aspect. 27
Viola. I think not so, my lord.
Duke.   Dear lad, believe it;
For they shall yet belie thy happy years,
That say thou art a man. Diana's lip 30
Is not more smooth and rubious; thy small pipe
Is as the maiden's organ, shrill and sound;
And all is semblative a woman's part 33
I know thy constellation is right apt 34
For this affair. Some four or five attend him,
All, if you will; for I myself am best
When least in company. Prosper well in this,
And thou shalt live as freely as thy lord,
To call his fortunes thine.
Viola.   I'll do my best
To woo your lady; [*Aside.*] yet, a barful strife! 40
Whoe'er I woo, myself would be his wife.
[*Exeunt.*

Scene five.

(OLIVIA'S HOUSE.)

Enter MARIA *and* Clown.

Maria. Nay, either tell me where thou hast been, or 1
I will not open my lips so wide as a bristle may enter in way of thy excuse. My lady will hang thee for thy absence.
Clown. Let her hang me; he that is well hanged in this world needs to fear no colours. 5
Maria. Make that good. 6
Clown. He shall see none to fear.

---

4. "humour": mood, temperament, disposition.

6. "inconstant": inconsistent or unreliable.

11. "aloof": waiting at some distance (out of earshot).

12-13. "unclasp'd . . . book": unfastened the book (metaphorical) of my innermost desires.

14. "gait": footsteps (walking).

15. "access": entrance.

20. "clamorous": noisy.

21. "unprofited return": do not return without accomplishing anything positive.

23. "unfold the passion of my love": foreign as the custom is to us in the 20th Century, wooing by proxy was often practised in Britain and Europe. The danger was that the proxy (the messenger) would reap personal advantage from the encounter.

24. "discourse": talk.

27. "nuncio's of more grave aspect": messenger's older and more serious appearance.

30. "Diana's lip": goddess' lip.

33. "semblative": resembling.

34. "constellation": zodiacal pattern.

40. "barful strife": obstacle that causes turmoil.
Notice that Viola is already in love with Orsino, but dare not reveal her identity.

1. "thou": Feste (the jester).

5. "fear no colours": fear no enemy (colors are regimental insignia or flags).

6. "Make that good": prove that.

TWELFTH NIGHT

ACT I SCENE V

The Clown is dressed in the traditional check costume and square hat with balls, and Maria is dressed as a rather comely kitchen maid. The two are in constant motion as they speak to one another, and there is an atmosphere of coquetting and flirtation which lightens the comedy.

They are evidently on excellent terms: the Clown calls Maria "as witty a piece of Eve's flesh as any in Illyria" and she calls him a "rogue" which is a compliment (in the circumstances). Maria announces the arrival of Countess Olivia, and the Clown puts his hands together in a mock prayer to Wit, to put him into good fooling. The Clown is having rather a difficult time amusing Olivia nowadays, since she has plunged herself into seven years' mourning.

Olivia now appears, looking very grave, and accompanied by her serious and pedantic steward, Malvolio. They are both dressed in black. They present a sight calculated to make any Clown weep! She no sooner sees the Clown then she sends him away, but he does not go. She says he is a dry fool and grows dishonest. He says that these are two faults that drink and good counsel will cure, and goes on to explain why. His explanation is highly illogical, and not very amusing (though long-winded).

To call attention to his reasoning in this argument, the Clown refers to his "simple syllogism" which, of course, it is not. The lady Olivia insists on his going away, but he claims there has been an error and asks her to give him permission to prove her a fool.

She does so, and he asks her certain questions in order to do so. The questions lead up to the fact that she believes her brother's soul is in heaven. So why mourn for him, then? demands the Clown. One should mourn for him only if he were in hell. This rather pleases Olivia, since it takes her out of herself. She asks Malvolio what he thinks of this fool, and the dour steward answers very contemptuously in the negative. He says the fool is infirm, and the Clown asks God to send Malvolio a speedy infirmity as a reward or, rather, punishment for speaking harshly of clowns.

Maria. A good lenten answer. I can tell thee where that saying was born, of "I fear no colours." 8

Clown. Where, good Mistress Mary?

Maria. In the wars; and that may you be bold to say in your foolery.

Clown. Well, God give them wisdom that have it; and those that are fools, let them use their talents.

Maria. Yet you will be hanged for being so long absent; or, to be turned away, is not that as good as a hanging to you?

Clown. Many a good hanging prevents a bad marriage; and, for turning away, let summer bear it out. 19

Maria. You are resolute, then? 20

Clown. Not so, neither; but I am resolved on two points. 22

Maria. That if one break, the other will hold; or, if both break, your gaskins fall. 24

Clown. Apt, in good faith, very apt. Well, go thy way; if Sir Toby would leave drinking, thou wert as witty a piece of Eve's flesh as any in Illyria.

Maria. Peace, you rogue, no more o' that. Here comes my lady. Make your excuse wisely, you were best.
　　　　　　　　　　　　　　　　　　　　[*Exit.*

Clown. Wit, an't be thy will, put me into good fooling! Those wits, that think they have thee, do very oft prove fools; and I, that am sure I lack thee, may pass for a wise man. For what says Quinapalus? 32 "Better a witty fool than a foolish wit."

　　　　Enter LADY OLIVIA *with* MALVOLIO.
God bless thee, lady! 33

Olivia. Take the fool away.

Clown. Do you not hear, fellows? Take away the lady.

Olivia. Go to, you're a dry fool; I'll no more of you. 36 Besides, you grow dishonest.

Clown. Two faults, madonna, that drink and good counsel will amend: for give the dry fool drink, then is the fool not dry; bid the dishonest man mend himself; if he mend, he is no longer dishonest; if he cannot, let the botcher mend him. Anything that's mended is but patched: virtue that transgresses is but patched with sin; and sin that amends is but patched with virtue. If that this simple syllogism will serve, 45 so; if it will not, what remedy? The lady bade take away the fool; therefore, I say again, take her away.

Olivia. Sir, I bade them take away you.

Clown. Misprision in the highest degree! Lady, cucul- 50 lus non facit monachum. That's as much to say as I 51 wear not motley in my brain. Good madonna, give me leave to prove you a fool.

Olivia. Can you do it?

Clown. Dexteriously, good madonna. 55

Olivia. Make your proof.

Clown. I must catechize you for it, madonna. Good 57 my mouse of virtue, answer me. 58

Olivia. Well, sir, for want of other idleness, I'll bide your proof.

Clown. Good madonna, why mournest thou?

Olivia. Good fool, for my brother's death.

Clown. I think his soul is in hell, madonna.

Olivia. I know his soul is in heaven, fool.

8. "lenten": short and spare (one fasts during the penitential season of Lent).

19. "for turning away . . .": that can be endured now that summer is coming in.

20. "resolute": resolved, determined.

22. "points": tagged lace for attaching hose to the doublet and fastening various parts where buttons came to be used.

24. "gaskins": breeches.

32. "Quinapalus": a fictitious, learned-sounding name.

33. Olivia's entrance is quite impressive; Malvolio precedes her, carrying his staff of office, and the maids-of-honor wait attentively in the background.

36. "dry fool": Olivia is in mourning and foolery ill becomes her at this time.

45. "syllogism": Feste, the jester, employs a kind of logical reasoning called the syllogism, consisting of the major and minor premises followed by a conclusion. His argument is a parody of the syllogistic method.

50-51. "Misprision": misunderstanding. "cucullus non facit monachum": the cowl does not make the monk.

55. "Dexteriously": neatly and skilfully.

57. "catechize": question formally.

58. "mouse": term of affection.

23

TWELFTH NIGHT
ACT I SCENE V

The Clown parries Malvolio's scornful judgment very neatly, and Olivia asks Malvolio what he thinks of the thrust. Malvolio answers that he marvels that his mistress can take delight in such a barren rascal. These fools can do nothing unless one serves them with an opening, and descends to their own level all the time to support the follow-up. He thinks wise men who do this are no better than Clowns' assistants. This shows how sour a man Malvolio really is. The Clown has little love for him.

Olivia says that Malvolio is sick of self-love, and cannot appreciate the taste of a good joke. He exaggerates everything and takes those little jokes intended for bird-bolts as if they were cannon-bullets. There is no harm in a professional Clown, though he do nothing but rail. The Clown praises Olivia for speaking well of fools, and Malvolio retires into himself yet farther.

Maria enters and says there is a young gentleman at the gate who desires admittance on a serious and important mission. We know that this must be Cesario (Viola in disguise).

Olivia senses he comes from the "Count." It should be pointed out that hitherto, Shakespeare has called Orsino Duke, but this fact evidently slipped his mind for here he uses the title Count to dignify Orsino. The mistake is insignificant, and should not be permitted to distract the student.

Olivia sends Malvolio to send the messenger away; Sir Toby has been delaying him in the interim. Sir Toby enters, half-drunk (as usual) and Olivia is disgusted with him. She asks who was at the gate, and Toby says he was a gentleman. Toby then lives up (or down) to his name by belching; he blames this on the pickled herring he has been eating, but drink is really responsible for his soused condition. He exits, neither knowing nor caring what is going on. Olivia and the Clown exchange remarks about the nature of a drunken man.

Olivia obviously likes her Clown's reply to her question for she sustains his answer in ordering him to

Clown. The more fool, madonna, to mourn for your brother's soul being in heaven. Take away the fool, gentlemen.

Olivia. What think you of this fool, Malvolio? doth he not mend? 68

Malvolio. Yes, and shall do till the pangs of death shake him. Infirmity, that decays the wise, doth ever make the better fool. 71

Clown. God send you sir, a speedy infirmity, for the better increasing your folly! Sir Toby will be sworn that I am no fox; but he will not pass his word for two pence that you are no fool.

Olivia. How say you to that, Malvolio?

Malvolio. I marvel your ladyship takes delight in such a barren rascal. I saw him put down the other day with an ordinary fool that has no more brain than a stone. Look you now, he's out of his guard already. Unless you laugh and minister occasion to him, he is gagged. I protest, I take these wise men, that crow so at these set kind of fools, no better than the fools' zanies. 78 84

Olivia. O, you are sick of self-love, Malvolio, and taste with a distempered appetite. To be generous, guiltless, and of free disposition, is to take those things for bird-bolts that you deem cannon-bullets. There is no slander in an allowed fool, though he do nothing but rail; nor no railing in a known discreet man, though he do nothing but reprove. 86 87 88 90

Clown. Now Mercury endue thee with leasing, for thou speakest well of fools! 92

Re-enter MARIA.

Maria. Madam, there is at the gate a young gentleman much desires to speak with you.

Olivia. From the Count Orsino, is it?

Maria. I know not, madam; 'tis a fair young man, and well attended.

Olivia. Who of my people hold him in delay?

Maria. Sir Toby, madam, your kinsman.

Olivia. Fetch him off, I pray you; he speaks nothing but madman; fie on him! [*Exit Maria.*] Go you, Malvolio. If it be a suit from the count, I am sick, or not at home—what you will, to dismiss it. [*Exit Malvolio.*] Now you see, sir, how your fooling grows old, and people dislike it. 103

Clown. Thou hast spoke for us, madonna, as if thy eldest son should be a fool, whose skull Jove cram with brains! for,—here he comes,—one of thy kin has a most weak pia mater. 107 108 110

Enter SIR TOBY.

Olivia. By mine honour, half drunk. What is he at the gate, cousin?

Sir Toby. A gentleman.

Olivia. A gentleman! what gentleman?

Sir Toby. 'Tis a gentleman here—a plague o' these pickle-herring! How now, sot! 115

Clown. Good Sir Toby!

Olivia. Cousin, cousin, how have you come so early by this lethargy? 119

Sir Toby. Lechery? I defy lechery. There's one at the gate. 120

68. "think you . . .": Olivia is pleased by the Clown's argument which touches her grief, but very delicately and inoffensively.

71. "Infirmity": Malvolio thinks the Clown is weak and sick; he is arrogant and scornful in his reply.

78. "barren rascal": Malvolio makes a withering reply, calling Feste 'a barren rascal.'
"put down": defeated (in jesting) by.

84. "fools' zanies": clowns' assistants.

86. "distempered": disordered.

87. "free disposition": generous outlook and manner.

88. "bird-bolts": blunt-headed arrows for shooting birds.

90. "rail": scold, revile, upbraid.

92. "Mercury": god of lies.
"leasing": the power of telling lies.

103. "suit": wooing.

107. "madonna": my lady.

107-108."as . . . fool": a reference to the proverb 'wise men have fools to their children.'

110. "pia mater": brain.

115. "pickle-herring": these have caused that indigestion for which Sir Toby's family name (Belch) is descriptive.

119. "lethargy": drowsiness.

120. "lechery": Sir Toby's tongue cannot get around the awkward th-sound in lethargy. Is this mispronunciation appropriate?

24

go and attend to Toby who is in the third degree of drink: he's drowned. (Hence the reference to the coroner.)

The Clown exits, and Malvolio re-enters; the young fellow at the gate swears he will speak with Olivia, and will not take no for an answer. He demands to be admitted, and will accept no excuse. Olivia is interested in this extraordinarily persistent youth. Yet she says, tell him he shall not speak with me. Malvolio reports that the youth has been told so, but swears he will stand at her door like a sheriff's messenger bearing a summons that must be delivered personally (thereby supporting the bench of magistrates, though a bench usually supports one when one sits upon it) but he'll speak with her.

The rather vague description of the youth given her by Malvolio whets Olivia's imagination, and she very much desires to see him, but is anxious not to reveal this and lose face in view of her previous adamant denial of access.

On hearing that the youth is very well-favored (good looking) Olivia says that he is to be allowed to approach her, and she calls a waiting gentlewoman to accompany her and sit in on the interview. She throws a veil over her face, and prepares to listen (once more) to Orsino's embassy.

Cesario enters (really Viola in disguise) and launches into a prepared speech in high poetic style. But he falters when it comes to addressing one of the two ladies present, since he does not know which is the lady of the house. Olivia says that he should speak to her; she will answer for the lady of the house. This equivocal reply puts Cesario off, and he says he hopes he is speaking to the right person for he has prepared a speech, and does not want to waste it for he spent lots of time and trouble learning it.

Olivia questions Cesario further. She wonders whether he is a comedian (comic actor) since he is so unwilling to speak except the part he has prepared by heart. An amusing and ambiguous exchange centering on their respective identities now takes place. Cesario is not the character he plays. Olivia is indeed the lady of the house "if," as she says, she does not "usurp" herself.

Cesario says if she is the lady Olivia, she does usurp herself; for what is hers to give away is not hers to retain. But he will go on with his speech in her praise, then come to the heart of the message. Note the play on "heart." It is a love-message, and addressed to the heart, or core.

Olivia. Ay, marry, what is he?

Sir Toby. Let him be the devil, an he will, I care not. Give me faith, say I. Well, it's all one.   [*Exit.*

Olivia. What's a drunken man like, fool?

Clown. Like a drowned man, a fool, and a madman: one draught above heat makes a fool; the second mads him; and a third drowns him.

Olivia. Go thou and seek the crowner, and let him sit o' my coz; for he's in the third degree of drink, he's drowned. Go, look after him.   128
129

Clown. He is but mad yet, madonna; and the fool shall look to the madman.   [*Exit.*

Re-enter MALVOLIO.

Malvolio. Madam, yond young fellow swears he will speak with you. I told him you were sick; he takes on him to understand so much, and therefore comes to speak with you. I told him you were asleep; he seems to have a foreknowledge of that too, and therefore comes to speak with you. What is to be said to him, lady? he's fortified against any denial.

Olivia. Tell him he shall not speak with me.

Malvolio. Has been told so; and he says, he'll stand at your door like a sheriff's post, and be the supporter to a bench, but he'll speak with you.   141
142

Olivia. What kind o' man is he?

Malvolio. Why, of mankind.

Olivia. What manner of man?

Malvolio. Of very ill manner; he'll speak with you, will you or no.

Olivia. Of what personage and years is he?

Malvolio. Not yet old enough for a man, nor young enough for a boy; as a squash is before 'tis a peascod, or a codling when 'tis almost an apple. 'Tis with him in standing water, between boy and man. He is very well favoured and he speaks very shrewishly; one would think his mother's milk were scarce out of him.   151
152
153
154

Olivia. Let him approach. Call in my gentlewoman.

Malvolio. Gentlewoman, my lady calls.   [*Exit.*

Re-enter MARIA.

Olivia. Give me my veil. Come throw it o'er my face. We'll once more hear Orsino's embassy.   159

Enter VIOLA and Attendants.

Viola. The honourable lady of the house, which is she?

Olivia. Speak to me; I shall answer for her. Your will?

Viola. Most radiant, exquisite and unmatchable beauty,—I pray you, tell me if this be the lady of the house, for I never saw her. I would be loath to cast away my speech, for besides that it is excellently well penned, I have taken great pains to con it. Good beauties, let me sustain no scorn; I am very comptible, even to the least sinister usage.   164
166
168

Olivia. Whence came you sir?

Viola. I can say little more than I have studied, and that question's out of my part. Good gentle one, give me modest assurance if you be the lady of the house, that I may proceed in my speech.

Olivia. Are you a comedian?

Viola. No my profound heart; and yet by the very fangs of malice I swear, I am not that I play.   176

128. "crowner": coroner (one who conducts inquests).

129. "sit": technical term applied to the holding of an inquest.

141. "sheriff's post": a sheriff's notice-board or messenger bearing notices of wanted men, rewards, proclamations etc.

142. "bench": magistrates' bench in court, or wooden seat.

151. "squash . . . peascod": unripe peascod before it becomes mature (leguminous vegetable).

152. "codling . . . apple": half-grown apple before it reaches full size.

153. "standing water": at the turn of the tide.

154. "shrewishly": scoldingly, in a bad-tempered manner, sharply.

159. "embassy": message (a diplomatic term) carried by an ambassador, or nuncio, in this case, Cesario.

164. "loath": reluctant.

166. "con": construe or learn by heart.

168. "comptible": sensitive.
"sinister usage": unfavorable treatment.

176. "play": Note the sustaining of the thought relating to the disguise of Viola.

TWELFTH NIGHT

ACT I SCENE V

Olivia asks Cesario to skip the praise part; it is likely to be false. She asks for an explanation of his sauciness at her gate. If he is mad, begone; if he has a reason, let it be brief. She does not want to waste any more time on so skipping a dialogue.

Maria, the maid, comes forward at this point to protect her mistress, and tells Cesario to hoist sail (a vulgar way of saying get out). Cesario says no; he intends to hull here a little longer. This effectively crushes the servant, and Cesario again addresses himself to Olivia.

Olivia asks him to speak his mind, but he declares he is a messenger. He must speak his master's mind. Olivia is scared that he has some hideous message to deliver since the formalities accompanying it are so fearful.

Cesario makes a lovely and reassuring speech saying that he holds the olive, the sign of peace, in his hand.

Olivia says, you began rudely; what do you want, and who are you?

Cesario explains that he had to be rude because he was rudely received by her people (especially Sir Toby). What he has to say is for her ears alone; it is as secret as maidenhead. Olivia immediately asks her attendants to withdraw; she will listen to this "divinity" (she uses the word ironically).

Now that he has the opportunity, Cesario does his level best to communicate his master's love to Olivia. He asks to see her face, and Olivia removes the veil. He praises its complexion and appearance in a truly delightful speech beginning "Tis beauty truly blent . . .." There is such passionate intensity in his pleading that Olivia is struck, not so much by the message (which is old and tired) but by the messenger (who is new, and young, and passionate).

Olivia listens with a certain detachment; her reply when she says her beauty shall be scheduled and inventoried (like goods for sale in a store) is rather sardonically cynical. Cesario senses that Olivia is too proud to be wooed by proxy. She is loved, Cesario tells her, by his lord and master; does this mean nothing to her? How can she be so hard-hearted? Olivia

Are you the lady of the house?

Olivia. If I do not usurp myself, I am.   178

Viola. Most certain, if you are she, you do usurp yourself; for what is yours to bestow is not yours to reserve. But this is from my commission. I will on with my speech in your praise, and then show you the heart of my message.

Olivia. Come to what is important in't; I forgive you the praise.

Viola. Alas, I took great pains to study it, and 'tis poetical.

Olivia. It is the more like to be feigned; I pray you, keep it in. I heard you were saucy at my gates, and allowed your approach rather to wonder at you than to hear you. If you be not mad, be gone; if you have reason, be brief. 'Tis not that time of moon with me to make one in so skipping a dialogue.   186 187

Maria. Will you hoist sail, sir? here lies your way.   192

Viola. No, good swabber; I am to hull here a little longer. Some mollification for your giant, sweet lady. Tell me your mind, I am a messenger.   193 194

Olivia. Sure, you have some hideous matter to deliver, when the courtesy of it is so fearful. Speak your office.

Viola. It alone concerns your ear. I bring no overture of war, no taxation of homage. I hold the olive in my hand; my words are as full of peace as matter.   199

Olivia. Yet you began rudely. What are you? what would you?   201

Viola. The rudeness that hath appeared in me have I learned from my entertainment. What I am, and what I would, are as secret as maidenhead; to your ears, divinity; to any other's, profanation.   204 205 206

Olivia. Give us the place alone; we will hear this divinity.   [*Exeunt* MARIA *and* Attendants.   207
Now, sir, what is your text?   208

Viola. Most sweet lady,—

Olivia. A comfortable doctrine, and much may be said of it. Where lies your text?   210

Viola. In Orsino's bosom.

Olivia. In his bosom! In what chapter of his bosom?

Viola. To answer by the method, in the first of his heart.   214

Olivia. Oh, I have read it; it is heresy. Have you no more to say?   215

Viola. Good madam, let me see your face.

Olivia. Have you any commission from your lord to negotiate with my face? You are now out of your text; but we will draw the curtain and show you the picture. Look you, sir, such a one I was this present. Is't not well done?   [*Unveiling.*   218 219 220

Viola. Excellently done, if God did all.

Olivia. 'Tis in grain sir; 'twill endure wind and weather.   224

Viola. 'Tis beauty truly blent, whose red and white Nature's own sweet and cunning hand laid on.
Lady, you are the cruell'st she alive,   227
If you will lead these graces to the grave

178. "usurp": Olivia has been keeping Cesario guessing about her identity until now, but does not realize that Cesario has been hiding her identity, and continues to hide it.

186. "feigned": false imitation, counterfeited.

187. "saucy": impudent.

192. "hoist sail": note the nautical metaphor.

193. "swabber": deck-washer.
"hull": moor.
Note how neatly Cesario retorts, turning Maria's metaphor back to her.

194. "giant": ironic hyperbole. Maria was small.

199. "olive": symbol of peace.

201. "rudely": crudely, awkwardly.
"what would you": what do you want?

204. "my entertainment": the manner in which I was received by your servants.

205. "maidenhead": virginity.

206. "profanation": violation.

207. Olivia echoes Viola's word, "divinity," yet with a trace of irony or even malice.

208. "text": sustains the image of "divinity" (suggests the Bible!).

210. "comfortable doctrine": sustains the idea of preaching from the text such divinity.

214. chapter and verse are ironically cited.

215. "heresy": unorthodox teaching condemned by the ordinary church.

218. "commission": order.

219. "out of your text": beyond the limits of your job.

220. "curtain": veil (suggests the picture of her face).

224. "in grain": natural (part of the wood, not painted on).

227. "she": lady.

TWELFTH NIGHT

ACT I SCENE V

asks how Orsino loves her, and receives a very passionate reply. The Countess says she cannot love Orsino, though she is aware of his many good points. He might have taken his answer (negative) long since.

Cesario says if he loved her with such a flaming ardor as Orsino does, he would not find any sense in this negative answer; he would not understand it.

Olivia is moved by the youth's passionate utterance. Why, what would you do, she asks. Cesario would not rest until the person that he loved at least felt pity for him. Olivia is impressed, and asks what the youth's parents were. Cesario assures her that he is a gentleman. She says go back to your lord and tell him I cannot love him. He must send no more. But if you wish to come here again, to tell me how he takes it, I will be glad to see you again. She hands him her purse full of money to spend for her. Cesario refuses the gift, indignantly. He is no fee-accepting person; his master, not himself, lacks reward. He leaves, calling her "fair cruelty."

After Cesario has left, Olivia remembers this conversation, and savors his replies on her tongue. She is aware that she is imperceptibly falling in love with the boy, and wonders whether, perhaps, the master (Orsino) were playing the man (Cesario). She means to find out. Sending for

And leave the world no copy.

Olivia. Oh, sir, I will not be so hard-hearted; I will give out divers schedules of my beauty. It shall be 231 inventoried, and every particle and utensil labelled 232 to my will: as, item, two lips, indifferent red; item, two grey eyes, with lids to them; item, one neck, one chin, and so forth. Were you sent hither to praise 235 me?

Viola. I see you what you are, you are too proud;
But, if you were the devil, you are fair.
My lord and master loves you. O, such love
Could be but recompensed, though you were crown'd
The nonpareil of beauty!   240

Olivia.   How does he love me?

Viola. With adorations, fertile tears,   241
With groans that thunder love, with sighs of fire.

Olivia. Your lord does know my mind. I cannot love him;
Yet I suppose him virtuous, know him noble,
Of great estate, of fresh and stainless youth;
In voices well divulged, free, learn'd and valiant;
And in dimension and the shape of nature
A gracious person: but yet I cannot love him;
He might have took his answer long ago.   249

Viola. If I did love you in my master's flame,   250
With such a suffering, such a deadly life,
In your denial I would find no sense;
I would not understand it.   253

Olivia.   Why, what would you?

Viola. Make me a willow cabin at your gate,   254
And call upon my soul within the house;
Write loyal cantons of contemned love   256
And sing them loud even in the dead of night;
Halloo your name to the reverberate hills,
And make the babbling gossip of the air
Cry out "Olivia!" Oh, you should not rest
Between the elements of air and earth,
But you should pity me!

Olivia.   You might do much.   262
What is your parentage?   263

Viola. Above my fortunes, yet my state is well;
I am a gentleman.

Olivia.   Get you to your lord;
I cannot love him. Let him send no more;
Unless, perchance, you come to me again,   267
To tell me how he takes it. Fare you well.
I thank you for your pains; spend this for me.   269

Viola. I am no fee'd post, lady; keep your purse.   270
My master, not myself, lacks recompense.   271
Love make his heart of flint that you shall love;
And let your fervour, like my master's, be
Placed in contempt! Farewell, fair cruelty. [*Exit.*

Olivia. "What is your parentage?"
"Above my fortunes, yet my state is well;
I am a gentleman." I'll be sworn thou art.
Thy tongue, thy face, thy limbs, actions, and spirit,
Do give thee five-fold blazon. Not too fast: soft, 279
        soft!
Unless the master were the man. How now!   280

231. "divers schedules": various lists.

232. "inventoried": itemized in a list, counted item by item.

235. "Were you sent . . . ?": Note the change of tone from cynical indifference to passionate resentment.

240. "nonpareil": without equal or parallel.

241. Note this perfect description of the rhetorical and superficial nature of Duke Orsino's love.

249. "He might have took": he might have taken.

250. "flame": passion or ardor.

253. "I would not . . . ": I would refuse to allow it to make sense to me.

254. "willow cabin": small hut with willow (the sign of unrequited love) before it.

256. "cantons": love songs (cantos). "contemned love": love that is given but not returned.

254-62. The impression of hallooing, reverberating, and babbling gossip is very brilliantly and masterfully created in this passage by the use of vowel sounds, assonance, and alliterative onomatopoeia.

263. "What is your parentage?": Olivia suspects that Cesario is of gentle birth.

267. "Unless, perchance, you come . . .": Olivia really desires this very much, but makes it sound casual.

269. "pains": trouble.

270. "no fee'd post": no paid messenger.

271. "recompense": reward.

279. "blazon": proclamation (like a coat-of-arms, or possibly, a triumphant blast on the trumpet).

280. "master": Orsino. "the man": the messenger.

TWELFTH NIGHT

ACT I SCENE V

Malvolio, she tells him to run after "that same peevish messenger" from the Duke, and return him the ring he left behind. We know, of course, that this is a trick because Cesario left no such thing behind. She wll explain this if the boy comes again tomorrow. She tells Malvolio to hurry off and do this, and he goes.

Olivia is in a delicious state of incipient love. She accepts her fate, whatever it may be, and goes out thinking of Cesario in the warmest terms.

The situation is complicated: the Countess loves a girl (Viola) masquerading as a boy (Cesario) while the Duke Orsino loves the Countess, who rejects him, and is in turn loved by a girl (Viola) who, to the Duke, is merely a serving-youth. How will it turn out?

Even so quickly may one catch the plague?
Methinks I feel this youth's perfections
With an invisible and subtle stealth
To creep in at mine eyes. Well, let it be.
What ho, Malvolio!

Re-enter MALVOLIO.

Malvolio. Here, madam, at your service.

Olivia. Run after that same peevish messenger, 286
The county's man. He left this ring behind him,
Would I or not. Tell him I'll none of it.
Desire him not to flatter with his lord,
Nor hold him up with hopes; I am not for him.
If that the youth will come this way to-morrow,
I'll give him reasons for't. Hie thee, Malvolio. 292

Malvolio. Madam, I will. [*Exit.*

Olivia. I do I know not what, and fear to find
Mine eye too great a flatterer for my mind
Fate, show thy force; ourselves we do not owe. 296
What is decreed must be, and be this so. [*Exit.*

286. "peevish": to the servants Cesario had been cross and fretful. Olivia keeps up this pretense to avoid letting Malvolio suspect that she, the countess, has fallen in love with Cesario.

292. "Hie thee": hurry up.

296. "ourselves we do not owe": Olivia is a fatalist; what is laid down for her (decreed) will happen. ·

ACT TWO, *scene one.*

(THE SEA-COAST.)

Enter ANTONIO *and* SEBASTIAN.

Antonio. Will you stay no longer? nor will you not   1
that I go with you?

Sebastian. By your patience, no. My stars shine
darkly over me. The malignancy of my fate might   4
perhaps distemper yours; therefore I shall crave of   5
you your leave that I may bear my evils alone. It were
a bad recompense for your love, to lay any of them
on you.

Antonio. Let me know of you whither you are bound.

Sebastian. No, sooth, sir. My determinate voyage is   9
mere extravagancy. But I perceive in you so excel-   10
lent a touch of modesty, that you will not extort
from me what I am willing to keep in; therefore it
charges me in manners the rather to express myself.
You must know of me then, Antonio, my name is
Sebastian, which I called Roderigo. My father was
that Sebastian of Messaline, whom I know you have   16
heard of. He left behind him myself and a sister,
both born in an hour. If the heavens had been
pleased, would we had so ended! but you, sir, altered
that; for some hour before you took me from the
breach of the sea was my sister drowned.

Antonio. Alas the day!

Sebastian. A lady, sir, though it was said she much
resembled me, was yet of many accounted beautiful;   23
but, though I could not with such estimable wonder
overfar believe that, yet thus far I will boldly pub-
lish her; she bore a mind that envy could not but
call fair. She is drowned already, sir, with salt water,
though I seem to drown her remembrance again
with more.

Antonio. Pardon me, sir, your bad entertainment.   29

Sebastian. O good Antonio, forgive me your trouble.

Antonio. If you will not murder me for my love, let
me be your servant.

Sebastian. If you will not undo what you have done,
that is, kill him whom you have recovered, desire it
not. Fare ye well at once: my bosom is full of kindness, and I am yet so near the manners of my mother,
that upon the least occasion more mine eyes will tell
tales of me. I am bound to the Count Orsino's
court. Farewell.   [*Exit.*

Antonio. The gentleness of all the gods go with
    thee!

I have many enemies in Orsino's court,
Else would I very shortly see thee there.
But, come what may, I do adore thee so,
That danger shall seem sport, and I will go.

    [*Exit.*

The scene changes to the sea-coast on another part of the land of Illyria, where we meet two more survivors of the shipwreck. They are Sebastian, a young gentleman, and the sea-captain, Antonio. They seem to be good friends in adversity. Sebastian has lost a twin-sister in the recent wreck. Sebastian himself almost perished but was rescued from the flood by the faithful sea-captain.

Sebastian wishes to visit the neighboring city, but Antonio dares not go there else he might be arrested, and he does not want to get Sebastian into trouble with the Illyrian authorities.

Sebastian describes his (presumed) dead twin-sister; she resembled him (this point comes up later) yet was by many accounted beautiful. Antonio is moved by his friend's grief but warns him that he is bad entertainment. He offers to be Sebastian's servant; Sebastian refuses this offer, and goes off to visit the court of Count Orsino.

Antonio fears to go there since he has many enemies at Orsino's court, but his valor overcomes his discretion and he does go. He follows Sebastian, probably with the intention of keeping the young gentleman out of trouble.

---

1. "nor . . . not": a double negative was permissible in Elizabethan English for the sake of emphasis.

4. "malignancy of my fate": the evil course of my destiny.

5. "distemper yours": spread like an illness and upset yours.

9. "determinate voyage": the journey I plan to make.

10. "mere extravagancy": only for recreation.

16. "Messaline": probably based on the Latin Massiliensis, Fr. Marseilles.

23. Note the contrast between Sebastian's commonsensical, calm, balanced, measured sentences, and Viola's poetic flights of passion.

29. "your bad entertainment": either spare me your mournful conversation, or forgive me for saying so, but you are poor entertainment with all this mournful talk.
This is the place to comment on the different uses to which prose and poetry are put in this play.
The love scenes are always in poetry. The straight conversation between Sebastian and Antonio (though full of fine masculine friendship) are not given the heightened qualities of verse.

You will recall that, at the end of Scene 5 in Act I, Olivia sent Malvolio after Cesario (Viola) to return the ring that Cesario did not leave with her. In this scene we see Malvolio talking to the youth in a very scornful, arrogant manner. He has the ring on the end of a long staff. He proffers it to Cesario, who is naturally astonished, and refuses the ring. At this Malvolio peevishly throws it down in front of Cesario, and stalks off.

Cesario is puzzled by this action. He left no ring with Olivia; what does she mean by returning it to him? "Fortune forbid my outside have not charm'd her," he says. Then he concludes: "She loves me, sure; the cunning of her passion invites me in this churlish messenger" (Malvolio). He hates to deceive Olivia, but dares not run the risk of undeceiving the Duke.

Cesario feels profoundly sorry for Olivia: "Poor lady, she were better love a dream" than to love me (Viola). Her disguise is succeeding only too well; it is an enemy in which "the pregnant enemy does much." Yet she must retain her disguise because, as a girl alone in a foreign country, she would be powerless to defend herself. (Remember, this was not the twentieth-century, and young ladies were not in the habit of traveling abroad alone and unprotected.)

There is a dreadfully complicated knot to be untangled. Viola loves her master; Orsino loves Olivia; Olivia loves Viola. Poor Viola leaves the knot to Time to untangle; it is too much for her.

ACT II SCENE III

At Olivia's house (downstairs), Sir Toby and Sir Andrew are carousing in drunken, noisy celebration. They are being waited on by Maria, who enjoys this noise-making, and the Clown soon joins them. They talk a lot of high-spirited (and high-sounding) non-

---

Scene two.

(A STREET.)

Enter VIOLA, MALVOLIO *following.*

Malvolio. Were not you even now with the Countess Olivia?

Viola. Even now, sir; on a moderate pace I have since arrived but hither.

Malvolio. She returns this ring to you, sir. You 5
might have saved me my pains, to have taken it away yourself. She adds, moreover, that you should put your lord into a desperate assurance she will none of him; and one thing more, that you be never so hardy to come again in his affairs, unless it be to report your lord's taking of this. Receive it so.

Viola. She took the ring of me; I'll none of it.

Malvolio. Come, sir, you peevishly threw it to her; and her will is, it should be so returned. If it be 14
worth stooping for, there it lies in your eye; if not, be it his that finds it.   [*Exit.*

Viola. I left no ring with her. What means this lady?
Fortune forbid my outside have not charm'd her! 17
She made good view of me; indeed, so much
That sure methought her eyes had lost her tongue,
For she did speak in starts distractedly.
She loves me, sure; the cunning of her passion
Invites me in this churlish messenger.
None of my lord's ring! why, he sent her none.
I am the man. If it be so, as 'tis,   24
Poor lady, she were better love a dream.   25
Disguise, I see, thou art a wickedness,   26
Wherein the pregnant enemy does much.
How easy is it for the proper-false
In women's waxen hearts to set their forms!
Alas, our frailty is the cause, not we!   30
For such as we are made of, such we be.
How will this fadge? my master loves her dearly;   32
And I, poor monster, fond as much on him;
And she, mistaken, seems to dote on me.
What will become of this? As I am man,
My state is desperate for my master's love;
As I am woman,—now alas the day!—
What thriftless sighs shall poor Olivia breathe!   38
O Time, thou must untangle this, not I!   39
It is too hard a knot for me to untie!   [*Exit.* 40

Scene three.

(OLIVIA'S HOUSE.)

Enter SIR TOBY *and* SIR ANDREW.

Sir Toby. Approach, Sir Andrew. Not to be a-bed after midnight is to be up betimes; and "diluculo 2
surgere," thou know'st,—   3

---

5. "returns this ring": Olivia's ruse to give Cesario a tangible reason for returning. Note the high-handed manner in which Malvolio addresses the messenger.

14. "so returned": i.e., peevishly (so Malvolio throws the ring down upon the floor, although some actors put the ring on the end of the staff of office and wave it at the messenger).

17. "Fortune forbid my outside have not charm'd her!": please God Olivia has not fallen in love with my outside (false) appearance.

24. "I am the man": Cesario realizes that Olivia has, indeed, fallen for himself rather than for his master.

25. "Poor lady . . .": Olivia is pitiable in her predicament.

26. "wickedness": Cesario speaks with feeling about the "wickedness" that arises from women's being deceived (since Eve) by disguise.

30. "frailty": The distinction between "frailty" and the woman who is frail is a subtle one.

32. "fadge": fall into place.

38. "thriftless sighs": extravagant and unprofitable sighs.

39. "O Time": an apostrophe to time (personified).

40. "knot": metaphorical expression of the complication of events so far.

2-3. "diluculo surgere": to rise early . . . (saluberrimum est) is the most healthy.
Sir Toby and Sir Andrew are returning to Olivia's house early in the morning, befuddled with wine.

TWELFTH NIGHT
ACT II SCENE III

sense, which our notes explain as far as this nonsense needs explaining. The mood is one of partying and manly indulgence. Marian (i.e., Maria) is keeping a lookout for she knows that Olivia is against these celebrations taking place in her own household, especially at this time.

Drunken parties soon encourage sing-songs, and this one is no exception. Sir Andrew calls for a song, and Sir Toby offers sixpence for one. Sir Andrew offers a testril too, and the Clown pockets both coins. He asks them what sort of a song they fancy, and they clamor for a love song rather than for a song of good life.

The Clown then sings an enchantingly melancholy love song, beginning "O mistress mine." In stage productions, the music by Roger Quilter is frequently used, although many composers have also set this song to music.

They listen intently, shaking their beer and wine glasses in time with the tune, and praise the Clown's singing at the end.

After the song, they clamor for a catch or what some of us might call a round. Everybody commences singing the same song, beginning at three or four different times, so that an interesting musical effect is achieved. The catch they want to sing here is "Hold thy peace, thou knave." It is a splendid opportunity for making an unholy (and probably most unmusical) row, and they are warming up to it beautifully.

Sir Andrew. Nay, by my troth, I know not; but I know, to be up late is to be up late.

Sir Toby. A false conclusion. I hate it as an unfilled can. To be up after midnight and to go to bed then, is early; so that to go to bed after midnight is to go to bed betimes. Does not our life consist of the four elements? 8 9

Sir Andrew. Faith, so they say; but I think it rather consists of eating and drinking.

Sir Toby. Thou'rt a scholar; let us therefore eat and drink. Marian, I say! a stoup of wine! 12 13

Enter Clown.

Sir Andrew. Here comes the fool, i' faith.

Clown. How now, my hearts! did you never see the picture of "We three"? 16

Sir Toby. Welcome, ass. Now let's have a catch. 17

Sir Andrew. By my troth, the fool has an excellent breast. I had rather than forty shillings I had such a leg, and so sweet a breath to sing, as the fool has. In sooth, thou wast in very gracious fooling last night, when thou spokest of Pigrogromitus, of the Vapians passing the equinoctial of Queubus. 'Twas very good, i' faith. I sent thee sixpence for thy leman. Hadst it? 22 24

Clown. I did impeticos thy gratillity: for Malvolio's nose is no whipstock; my lady has a white hand, and the Myrmidons are no bottle-ale houses. 25 27

Sir Andrew. Excellent! why, this is the best fooling, when all is done. Now, a song.

Sir Toby. Come on; there is sixpence for you—let's have a song.

Sir Andrew. There's a testril of me too. If one knight give a— 32

Clown. Would you have a love song, or a song of good life?

Sir Toby. A love song, a love song.

Sir Andrew. Ay, ay. I care not for good life.

Clown. [*Sings*]

> O mistress mine, where are you roaming? 36
> O, stay and hear; your true love's coming,
> That can sing both high and low.
> Trip no further, pretty sweeting;
> Journeys end in lovers meeting,
> Every wise man's son doth know.

Sir Andrew. Excellent good, i' faith.

Sir Toby. Good, good.

Clown [*Sings*]

> What is love? 'tis not hereafter;
> Present mirth hath present laughter;
> What's to come is still unsure.
> In delay there lies no plenty;
> Then come kiss me, sweet and twenty,
> Youth's a stuff will not endure.

Sir Andrew. A mellifluous voice, as I am true knight. 50

Sir Toby. A contagious breath. 51

Sir Andrew. Very sweet and contagious, i' faith.

Sir Toby. To hear by the nose, it is dulcet in contagion. But shall we make the welkin dance indeed? shall we rouse the night-owl in a catch that will draw three souls out of one weaver? shall we do that? 53 54 56

8-9. "four elements": earth, air, fire, and water: the Elizabethans believed that humanity was made up of various combinations of these four elements. The theory of humours was based upon this theory.

12. "scholar": ironic, for Sir Andrew cannot remember the lessons that are echoed and parodied by Sir Toby in this scene.

13. "Marian": affectionate variation on Maria.
"stoup": cup, flagon, or tankard.

16. "We three": picture of two donkeys; the viewer made up the third! Sir Toby knows this joke, for he calls the Clown the third ("ass").

17. "catch": musical round.

22. "Pigrogromitus . . .": a fantastic story made up and told by Feste; (pigro = lazy, vap = vapid, Queubus = cubus [cube] or queue [tail]).

24. "leman": sweetheart.

25. "impeticos thy gratillity": I pocketed your tip myself, for Malvolio pokes his nose into my business, and my girl friend (who is a lady) and I go to the high-class Myrmidons taverns and not to mere lowdown pubs. Feste runs all this together, making paraphrase difficult.

27. "Myrmidons": a chain of high-class taverns in London, named after the warlike-race of Thessaly, whom Achilles led to the siege of Troy.

32. "testril": fanciful form of 'tester' = sixpence.

36. The lyric that follows is light and in keeping with the mood of the players and the atmosphere of the whole play. Certain it is that, as far as the disguise-theme of this play is concerned, "What's to come is still unsure." (l. 50)

50. "mellifluous": sweetly and smoothly flowing.

51. "contagious": means either an attractive song or bad breath.

53. "To hear by the nose . . .": If one could hear with one's nose this song would be sweetness in the midst of a strong foul smell.

54. "welkin": sky (used humorously here).

56. "three souls out of one weaver": weavers (usually Belgian refugees) were commonly regarded as being such miserable men, owing to their extreme thrift, that it would take nine of them to equal one ordinary, generous man!

TWELFTH NIGHT

ACT II SCENE III

They sing, or, rather, roar out this catch, and at the end Maria enters and warns them that my lady has probably sent for her steward Malvolio to turn them all out of doors. They are too far gone in their cups to care much, and call Olivia and Malvolio meaningless but unpleasant-sounding names. They start another catch, "There dwelt a man in Babylon, lady, lady." The uproar threatens to break out all over again.

All caution to the winds, they commence a third catch, "Oh, the twelfth day of December," when there is a warning cry or gasp from Maria, and Malvolio appears at the head of the stairs. He is a magnificently ridiculous figure, attired in his nightgown and nightcap (long, and tapering to a point), and carrying a lit candle in a candlestick. He has evidently been roused from sleep, and is in a foul temper. He feels his authority as steward has been flaunted. He asks them if they are mad, or what they are, that they gabble like tinkers at this time of night. Is there no respect of place, persons, or time in them?

Sir Toby said they did keep time in their catches (musical time, he means) but this humorous quibble is ignored. Malvolio is round with them: if they cannot separate themselves from their disorders, they must leave the lady Olivia's house even though Toby is her relative.

This reminds Toby of a fourth catch: "Farewell, dear heart, since I must needs be gone." Malvolio, scandalized, advances down the steps and steps into the large kitchen.

The Clown takes up this same tune, and they sing in Malvolio's very face. Finally, Malvolio turns to Maria and warns her that she should not let them use her lady's kitchens for such an uncivil display. He goes out, but not before they have blown out his candle and pulled his nightcap over his eyes. Maria tells him to shake his ears, and the cowardly Andrew threatens to challenge him to a duel and then make promise and fail to turn up, thereby making a fool of him. Toby says write the challenge in a war-like hand, or let him (Toby) deliver it to him by word of mouth.

Sir Andrew. An you love me, let's do't. I am dog at a catch. 57

Clown. By'r lady, sir, and some dogs will catch well.

Sir Andrew. Most certain. Let our catch be, "Thou knave."

Clown. "Hold thy peace, thou knave," knight? I shall be constrained in't to call thee knave, knight.

Sir Andrew. 'Tis not the first time I have constrained one to call me knave. Begin, fool. It begins "Hold thy peace."

Clown. I shall never begin if I hold my peace.

Sir Andrew. Good, i' faith. Come, begin.

[*Catch sung.*

Enter MARIA.

Maria. What a caterwauling do you keep here! If 66 my lady have not called up her steward Malvolio and bid him turn you out of doors, never trust me.

Sir Toby. My lady's a Catian, we are politicians, 69 Malvolio's a Peg-a-Ramsey, and "Three merry men 70 be we." Am not I consanguineous? am I not of her 71 blood? Tillyvally. Lady! [*Sings*] "There dwelt a man in Babylon, lady, lady!"

Clown. Beshrew me, the knight's in admirable fooling.

Sir Andrew. Ay, he does well enough if he be disposed, and so do I too. He does it with a better grace, but I do it more natural.

Sir Toby. [*Sings*] "Oh, the twelfth day of December,"—

Maria. For the love o' God, peace!

Enter MALVOLIO.

Malvolio. My masters, are you mad? or what are 80 you? Have you no wit, manners, nor honesty, but to gabble like tinkers at this time of night? Do ye make 82 an ale-house of my lady's house, that ye squeak out your coziers' catches without any mitigation or 84 remorse of voice? Is there no respect of place, persons, nor time in you?

Sir Toby. We did keep time, sir, in our catches. 86 Sneck up! 87

Malvolio. Sir Toby, I must be round with you. My lady bade me tell you, that, thought she harbours you as her kinsman, she's nothing allied to your disorders. If you can separate yourself and your mis- 90 demeanors, you are welcome to the house; if not, an it would please you to take leave of her, she is very willing to bid you farewell.

Sir Toby. "Farewell, dear heart, since I must needs be gone."

Maria. Nay, good Sir Toby.

Clown. "His eyes do show his days are almost done."

Malvolio. Is't even so?

Sir Toby. "But I will never die."

Clown. Sir Toby, there you lie.

Malvolio. This is much credit to you.

Sir Toby. "Shall I bid him go?" 100

Clown. "What an if you do?"

Sir Toby. "Shall I bid him go, and spare not?"

Clown. "Oh, no, no, no, no, you dare not!"

Sir Toby. Out o' tune, sir! ye lie. Art any more than 104

57. "dog at": clever at.

66. "caterwauling": making a wailing noise like a cat. From Middle English cat + wawen, to wail (an onomatopoetic word, whose sound echoes its meaning).

69. "Catian": native of Cathay (China), and hence a scoundrel, rogue, or sharper.

70. "Peg-a-Ramsey": the name of a song applied to Malvolio as a term of reproach by Sir Toby. The ballad, now lost, contains some refrains in which a henpecked husband longs for his bachelor days with the words: "Give me my yellow hose again, give me my yellow hose." This may have suggested the idea of yellow stockings for guying Malvolio to Shakespeare.

71. "consanguineous": related by blood.

80. "masters . . . mad": the alliteration of the m-consonant adds rhetorical force to this severe and outraged speech.

82. "tinkers": tinkers were a noisy lot and, being gypsies, had their own language (Romany).

84. "coziers'": cobblers'. "mitigation": softening of the sound.

86. "time . . . in our catches": short musical compositions for three or more voices, which sing the same melody, the second singer beginning the first line as the first goes on to the second line, and so on.

87. "Sneck up!": Go hang (onomatopoetic sound of a man's neck breaking).

90. "misdemeanors": faults.

100. "Shall I bid him go?": Toby and Feste alter the words of the ancient song to fit their present situation.

104-6. Toby addresses Feste, First; then, Malvolio.

Maria tells them to be quiet for she has an idea that will "gull him (Malvolio) into a nayword, and make him a common recreation."

Maria is confident that she can make a fool of Malvolio, and Sir Toby (taken by this idea, and excited at the prospect) demands to know how she is going to do it.

Malvolio takes himself very seriously and is a kind of puritan. She plans to drop in his path some obscure love-letters so designed and phrased that he will assume they are written to him by the Countess Olivia, and that she is in love with him. Maria can write like Olivia, and they all feel that this trick will trap Malvolio.

a steward? Dost thou think, because thou art vir- 105
tuous, there shall be no more cakes and ale? 106

Clown. Yes, by St. Anne, and ginger shall be hot i'
the mouth too.

Sir Toby. Thou'rt i' the right. Go, sir rub your chain 109
with crumbs. A stoup of wine, Maria!

Malvolio. Mistress Mary, if you prized my lady's
favour at anything more than contempt, you would
not give means for this uncivil rule. She shall 113
know of it, by this hand. [*Exit.*

Maria. Go shake your ears.

Sir Andrew. 'Twere as good a deed as to drink when
a man's a-hungry, to challenge him the field, and then
to break promise with him and make a fool of him. 118

Sir Toby. Do't, knight. I'll write thee a challenge; or
I'll deliver thy indignation to him by word of mouth.

Maria. Sweet Sir Toby, be patient for to-night. Since
the youth of the count's was to-day with my lady,
she is much out of quiet. For Monsieur Malvolio,
let me alone with him; if I do not gull him into a 124
nayword, and make him a common recreation, do 125
not think I have wit enough to lie straight in my
bed. I know I can do it.

Sir Toby. Possess us, possess us; tell us something
of him.

Maria. Marry, sir, sometimes he is a kind of puritan. 128

Sir Andrew. Oh, if I thought that, I'd beat him like 129
a dog.

Sir Toby. What, for being a puritan? thy exquisite 130
reason, dear knight.

Sir Andrew. I have no exquisite reason for't, but I
have reason good enough.

Maria. The devil a puritan that he is, or anything
constantly, but a time-pleaser; an affectioned ass, 135
that cons state without book and utters it by great 136
swarths: the best persuaded of himself, so crammed,
as he thinks, with excellencies, that it is his grounds
of faith that all that look on him love him; and on 139
that vice in him will my revenge find notable cause
to work.

Sir Toby. What wilt thou do?

Maria. I will drop in his way some obscure epistles 142
of love, wherein, by the colour of his beard, the shape
of his leg, the manner of his gait, the expressure of
his eye, forehead, and complexion, he shall find himself most feelingly personated. I can write very like 146
my lady your niece; on a forgotten matter we can
hardly make distinction of our hands.

Sir Toby. Excellent! I smell a device. 149

Sir Andrew. I have't in my nose too.

Sir Toby. He shall think, by the letters that thou wilt
drop, that they come from my niece, and that she's
in love with him.

Maria. My purpose is, indeed, a horse of that colour.

Sir Andrew. And your horse now would make him 155
an ass. 156

Maria. Ass, I doubt not.

Sir Andrew. Oh, 'twill be admirable!

Maria. Sport royal, I warrant you. I know my physic 159
will work with him. I will plant you two, and let the

105-6. "Dost thou think, because thou art virtuous, there shall be no more cakes and ale?": This is the classic challenge to puritans of every time and place. Why did the modern English novelist, Somerset Maughan, employ "CAKES AND ALE" as the title of a collection of some of his short stories?

109. "Go, Sir, rub your chain with crumbs": Addressed to the steward, Malvolio (referring to his chain of office which he wore around his neck like a mayoral chain).

113. "give means for": provide the opportunity for.

118. Andrew has the idea of challenging Malvolio to a duel; note that later he challenges Cesario with the idea of breaking challenge with him, but the trick does not work too successfully.

124. "gull him": deceive and trick him.

125. "nayword": byword.
"recreation": laughing-stock.

128. "puritan": member of a group in the Church of England during the 16th and 17th centuries who wanted simpler forms of worship and stricter morals (many puritans settled in New England). Hence, any person who is very strict in morals and religion (from Latin puritas, purity).

129. Sir Andrew misunderstands again!

130. "exquisite": exact or precise.

135. "affectioned": affected, one who puts on airs.

136. "cons state": learns passages on etiquette and politics by great chunks, and quotes them at length; a bore.

139. "all that look on him love him": Maria bases her "revenge" on Malvolio's excessive egotism.

142. "obscure epistles": letters that make sense but not clear or complete sense.

146. "feelingly personated": sympathetically impersonated or imitated.

149. "device": trick.

155-6. "horse . . . ass": one of Sir Andrew's happier jokes. How would he deliver it?

159. "physic": medicine (to cure his pride).

TWELFTH NIGHT

ACT II SCENE III

Even Sir Andrew likes the idea which is to make Malvolio think Olivia is in love with him. It will be sport royal! She plans to plant them where they will be able to see his construction of it. Then she bids them goodnight, and after her exit they are jubilant in praise of her and her trick. They call her a true-bred beagle and other country terms of endearment, and drink on a little longer. Sir Toby warns Andrew to send for more money. Toby goes off to burn some sack (heat some wine) because it is too late for him to go to bed now. He exits with Sir Andrew. "Come, knight; come, knight."

ACT II SCENE IV

At Orsino's Palace, music is again being played in the background, while the languid and indolent Duke asks for that old and antique song they heard last night. Feste, the Clown, is not there to sing it, however, so the Duke sends Curio to seek him. Meanwhile Orsino addresses Cesario (Viola) on the subject of how true lovers suffer. Cesario knows more than the Duke about the pangs of love and is able to describe them with a felicity that amazes him. We cannot help noticing that Viola's feelings are deeper and more sensitive than those of Orsino.

Shakespeare makes this distinction in the verse he gives the two characters: Orsino's verse is magnificent and rhetorical, the verse of public formal utterance; Viola speaks in verse that is private and inward-directed.

"Thou dost speak masterly," Orsino tells her; we know, of course, that her feelings are maidenly rather than masterly. He questions her about her own experience of love, and she describes a person of Orsino's complexion. Orsino believes that the man should be older than the girl, and he makes a telling observation about the giddiness and instability of men's fancies contrasted with women's.

---

fool make a third, where he shall find the letter. Observe his construction of it. For this night, to bed, 161 and dream on the event. Farewell.   [*Exit.*

Sir Toby. Good night, Penthesilea.   163

Sir Andrew. Before me, she's a good wench.

Sir Toby. She's a beagle, true-bred, and one that adores me. What o' that?

Sir Andrew. I was adored once too.

Sir Toby. Let's to bed, knight. Thou hadst need send 168
for more money.   169

Sir Andrew. If I cannot recover your niece, I am a 170
foul way out.

Sir Toby. Send for money, knight. If thou hast her
not i' the end, call me cut.   172

Sir Andrew. If I do not, never trust me, take it how
you will.

Sir Toby. Come, come, I'll go burn some sack; 'tis 174
too late to go to bed now. Come, knight; come,
knight.   [*Exeunt.*

Scene four.

(THE DUKE'S PALACE.)

Enter DUKE, VIOLA, CURIO, *and* Others.

Duke. Give me some music. Now, good-morrow, 1
    friends.
Now, good Cesario, but that piece of song,
That old and antique song we heard last night. 3
Methought it did relieve my passion much,
More than light airs and recollected terms 5
Of these most brisk and giddy-paced times. 6
Come, but one verse.

Curio. He is not here, so please your lordship, that
should sing it.

Duke. Who was it?

Curio. Feste, the jester, my lord; a fool that the lady 11
Olivia's father took much delight in. He is about the
house.

Duke. Seek him out, and play the tune the while.
    [*Exit* CURIO. *Music plays.*
Come hither, boy. If ever thou shalt love,
In the sweet pangs of it remember me;
For such as I am all true lovers are,
Unstaid and skittish in all motions else, 17
Save in the constant image of the creature
That is beloved. How dost thou like this tune?

Viola. It gives a very echo to the seat
Where Love is throned.

Duke.   Thou dost speak masterly. 21
My life upon't, young though thou art, thine eye
Hath stay'd upon some favour that it loves. 23
Hath it not, boy?

Viola.   A little, by your favour. 24

Duke. What kind of woman is't?

Viola.   Of your complexion. 25

Duke. She is not worth thee, then. What years, i' 26
    faith?

---

161. "construction": interpretation.

163. "Penthesilea": Queen of the Amazons, a race of female warriors. A reference to Maria's diminutive stature with, perhaps, an appreciative recognition of her spirited behavior.

168-9. "send for more money": Sir Andrew is footing the bills for their carousel.

170. "out": out of pocket.

172. "cut": cart-horse.

174. "burn some sack": heat some wine with sugar and spices (Is Sir Toby unwilling to go to bed, or incapable of going?).

1. "music": the signature-tune of Orsino.

3. "old and antique song": the Duke's musical taste seems to have been very conservative.

5-6. "more than light airs . . .": Is there some criticism of modern music here?

11. "Feste": Olivia's father delighted in Feste, the jester; which is why Olivia keeps him on.

17. "Unstaid and skittish": unstable and excitable motions, probably emotions.

21. "Love": here personified; If Orsino suffers (from unrequited passion), Viola also suffers from unrevealed love.
"masterly": like a master (note the masculine reference when we all know that Cesario is actually female).

23. "favour": girl (favored one).

24. "favour": permission (note the play on the word. Orsino is actually her favored one).

25. "your complexion": she really means you.

26. "What years": what age is she?

34

TWELFTH NIGHT

ACT II SCENE IV

This tender conversation about the nature of male and female love continues, and Viola closes it on a rather melancholy and hopeless note just before Curio and the Clown re-enter. The Duke prepares to hear some music that exactly fits his aesthetic mood. Now follows "Come away, come away, death," one of the sweetest of the Shakespearean love lyrics.

The free maids that sing this song are either unmarried girls, knitting, or else the three Parces, or Fates, weaving the thread of life and cutting it with scissors of mortality. The theme of the lyric is the sadness unto death of a young man whose love for a fair, cruel maid was unrequited. He dies of his love, and hopes that no other sad true lover shall find his grave, to weep there for similar reasons (unrequited love).

The theme of the song expresses Orsino's mood, and also that of Olivia, as well as that of Viola. All three love, and their love in each case is unrequited.

Orsino gives Feste some money for his singing. There is some verbal play on pains and pleasure. After an amusing speech expressing praise of his benefactor, the Clown exits. Cesario alone remains, and Orsino forthwith sends him (her) to Olivia, "yond same sovereign cruelty," to tell her that the Duke is interested in she herself, not in her landed possessions; he loves her truly.

Viola. About your years, my lord.
Duke. Too old, by heaven. Let still the woman take
An elder than herself; so wears she to him,
So sways she level in her husband's heart.
For, boy, however we do praise ourselves,
Our fancies are more giddy and unfirm,   32
More longing, wavering, sooner lost and worn,
Than women's are.
Viola.   I think it well, my lord.
Duke. Then let thy love be younger than thyself   35
Or thy affection cannot hold the bent;
For women are as roses, whose fair flower
Being once display'd, doth fall that very hour.
Viola. And so they are. Alas, that they are so;
To die, even when they to perfection grow!

Re-enter CURIO *and* Clown.

Duke. O fellow, come, the song we had last night.
Mark it, Cesario, it is old and plain;
The spinsters and the knitters in the sun,
And the free maids that weave their thread with
    bones
Do use to chant it. It is silly sooth,   45
And dallies with the innocence of love,   46
Like the old age.
Clown. Are you ready, sir?
Duke. Ay; prithee, sing.   [*Music.* 49

SONG

Clown. Come away, come away, death,
        And in sad cypress let me be laid;
    Fly away, fly away, breath;
        I am slain by a fair cruel maid.
    My shroud of white, stuck all with yew,
            O prepare it!
    My part of death, no one so true
            Did share it.

    Not a flower, not a flower sweet,
        On my black coffin let there be strown;
    Not a friend, not a friend greet
        My poor corpse, where my bones shall
            be thrown.
    A thousand thousand sighs to save,
            Lay me, oh, where
    Sad true lover never find my grave,
            To weep there!

Duke. There's for thy pains.   66
Clown. No pains, sir; I take pleasure in singing,
sir.
Duke. I'll pay thy pleasure then.
Clown. Truly, sir, and pleasure will be paid, one
time or another.
Duke. Give me now leave to leave thee.
Clown. Now, the melancholy god protect thee; and
the tailor make thy doublet of changeable taffeta, 73
for thy mind is a very opal. I would have men of   74
such constancy put to sea, that their business might
be everything and their intent everywhere; for that's
it that always makes a good voyage of nothing.
Farewell.   [*Exit.*

32. Orsino's point of view, that men's affections are less stable than women's, is soon contradicted by his view that women cannot love with the same passionate intensity and strength as men can.

35. Note the poetry in Orsino's description. It is moving though rhetorical, and contrasts with the poetry of Viola, which is less superficial, less formal, more sensitive, and finer than Orsino's. There is a wealth of melancholy in Viola's speech, whereas Orsino's speech is egotistic and sensual.

45. "silly sooth": simple truth.

46. "dallies": toys with.

49. "prithee": I entreat you.
The old and antique song, "Come away, come away, death," now follows. It is both ancient and quaint, or full of antics or conceits. Its melancholy artifice probably appeals to the Duke in his present mood, and certainly suits the musical atmosphere of the play as a whole.

66. "pains": trouble.

73. "changeable taffeta": shot silk which changes color as the light changes.

74. "opal": a gem with changeable colors according to the light.

TWELFTH NIGHT

ACT II SCENE IV

Cesario asks what "if she cannot love you, sir?" And Orsino says he cannot be so answered. Then Cesario puts the case to him in a different light.

Say that there is some lady who has as much love for Orsino as he has for Olivia: he cannot love this lady, and tells her so. Must she not then accept this answer?

Orsino denies the parallel. No woman could possibly love with so strong a passion as he loves. Women cannot restrain themselves. Their love is like an appetite. Therefore there should be no analogy between the love he bears Olivia and that any woman can bear him.

This is egotistical male nonsense, of course, and hurts Viola (but she cannot reveal the hurt). She knows too well what love women to men may bear. They are as true of heart as men (truer, we suspect, from her understatement). Cesario says her father had a daughter who loved a man as he, Cesario, might love Orsino were he (Cesario) a woman. She never told her love, but let the effort of concealing it destroy her good looks until she pined away in green and yellow melancholy, and sat like patience on a monument, smiling at grief.

Men may swear that they love more than women do, may talk more about their feelings: but their shows are mere empty professions not supported by the will. Men prove much by their vows, but little in the performance of them.

Orsino is touched enough to ask if the youth's sister died of her love. Viola gives a rather evasive answer, which does not really answer the question, and asks if she still has to go to Olivia.

Orsino says, yes. Go to her quickly. Give her this jewel. Tell her my love can give place to nobody; put up with no delay.

Duke. Let all the rest give place.   78
　　　　[CURIO *and* Attendants *retire.*
　　　　　　　Once more, Cesario,
Get thee to yond same sovereign cruelty.   79
Tell her, my love, more noble than the world,
Prizes not quantity of dirty lands;   81
The parts that fortune hath bestow'd upon her,
Tell her, I hold as giddily as fortune;
But 'tis that miracle and queen of gems,
That nature pranks her in, attracts my soul.   85
Viola. But if she cannot love you, sir?
Duke. I cannot be so answer'd.
　　　　　　　　　　　Sooth, but you must.   86
Say that some lady, as perhaps there is,
Hath for your love as great a pang of heart
As you have for Olivia. You cannot love her;
You tell her so; must she not then be answer'd?
Duke. There is no woman's sides   92
Can bide the beating of so strong a passion
As love doth give my heart; no woman's heart
So big, to hold so much. They lack retention.
Alas, their love may be called appetite,—
No motion of the liver, but the palate,—   97
That suffer surfeit, cloyment and revolt;   98
But mine is all as hungry as the sea,
And can digest as much. Make no compare
Between that love a woman can bear me
And that I owe Olivia.
Viola.　　　　　　Ay, but I know—
Duke. What dost thou know?
Viola. Too well what love women to men may owe.
In faith, they are as true of heart as we.
My father had a daughter loved a man,
As it might be, perhaps, were I a woman,
I should your lordship.
Duke.　　　　And what's her history?
Viola. A blank, my lord. She never told her love,
But let concealment, like a worm i' the bud,
Feed on her damask cheek. She pined in thought, 111
And with a green and yellow melancholy
She sat like patience on a monument,   113
Smiling at brief. Was not this love indeed?
We men may say more, swear more; but indeed
Our shows are more than will; for still we prove
Much in our vows, but little in our love.
Duke. But died thy sister of her love, my boy?
Viola. I am all the daughters of my father's house,
And all the brothers too; and yet I know not.   120
Sir, shall I to this lady?   121
Duke.　　　　　　Ay, that's the theme.
To her in haste; give her this jewel; say,
My love can give no place, bide no denay.   123
　　　　　　　　　　　　　　　[*Exeunt.*

78. "give place": leave us alone.

79. "yond": yonder.
"same sovereign cruelty": Olivia.

81. "prizes not quantity . . .": does not value her real estate.

85. "pranks": decorates.

86. "Sooth": truth or truly.

92. et seq., Orsino's advice on men's passion being less constant and intense than women's has one exception, evidently: himself.

97. "motion of the liver": the liver was regarded as the seat of the passions.
"palate": taste-buds in the mouth.

98. "suffer surfeit": experience an excess. (note the alliteration of the sibilant-s).
"cloyment": weary by too much of anything sweet and pleasant.

111. "damask": silky smooth as a Damascus rose.
"pined in thought": brooded over it.

113. "She sat like patience on a monument": a perfect simile to express calm endurance and waiting.

120. "and yet I know not": Viola is really talking about herself.

121. "shall I": (go again)
"to this lady": (Olivia).
"theme": main intent.

123. "denay": noun (substantive), old form of denial

36

TWELFTH NIGHT

ACT II SCENE V

One of the most comic scenes in the play now takes the stage: the gulling of Malvolio. Sir Toby Belch, Sir Andrew Aguecheek, and Fabian have met by arrangement in Olivia's garden. They are hoping that Malvolio, this "niggardly, rascally, sheep-biter" as Toby calls him, will soon come to "some notable shame." Fabian exults in the prospect, and says he would not lose a scruple of the sport: this is because he has a personal grudge against the steward, about bear-baiting. Now Malvolio is to be the bear, and they are about to bait (tease) him.

They intend to fool him "black and blue." Yet there is no genuine malevolence in their actions; they resent Malvolio's lack of human sympathy and his puritanical arrogance towards them. Because of this, we find it difficult to sympathize with Malvolio until the end of the play. He is like a man who looks down the wrong end of a telescope and sees everything in the world diminished in stature and at a great distance off.

Maria now enters, and tells them all three to hide in the box-tree. This was the yew-hedge cut square to resemble a box. Malvolio is coming down the walk. She throws down a letter on the path, where he is certain to find it. If this letter does not make a contemplative idiot of him, Maria implies, she has accomplished nothing.

Dressed in black and wearing his steward's chain of office, Malvolio enters, talking about Olivia. He is trying to persuade himself that his lady loves him. The other characters behind the box-hedge make rude and pertinent comments about him from time to time. On stage the timing has to be good so that Malvolio is seen to be unaware of the presence of these eavesdroppers and spectators.

The various movements and gestures of the comic characters, their interjections, gests, and evasions, taken with Malvolio's own egotistical pronouncements, form a complex structure that is very entertaining and utterly hilarious.

Malvolio is utterly oblivious of what is taking place behind his back, so lost is he in his vain contemplations. He imagines himself three months married to Olivia, sitting in his state, calling his officers about him in his branched velvet gown, having come from a day-bed where he has left the Countess sleeping.

Scene five.

(OLIVIA'S GARDEN.)

Enter SIR TOBY, SIR ANDREW, *and* FABIAN.

Sir Toby. Come thy ways, Signior Fabian. 1

Fabian. Nay, I'll come; if I lose a scruple of this 2
sport, let me be boiled to death with melancholy. 3

Sir Toby. Wouldst thou not be glad to have the niggardly rascally sheep-biter come by some notable 5
shame?

Fabian. I would exult, man. You know, he brought 6
me out o' favour with my lady about a bear-baiting 7
here.

Sir Toby. To anger him we'll have the bear again; 8
and we will fool him black and blue. Shall we not, 9
Sir Andrew?

Sir Andrew. An we do not, it is pity of our lives.

Sir Toby. Here comes the little villain.

Enter MARIA.

How now, my metal of India! 12

Maria. Get ye all three into the box-tree. Malvolio's
coming down this walk. He has been yonder i' the
sun practising behaviour to his own shadow this
half-hour. Observe him, for the love of mockery;
for I know this letter will make a contemplative 17
idiot of him. Close, in the name of jesting! Lie thou
there [*throws down a letter*]; for here comes the
trout that must be caught with tickling. [*Exit.* 20

Enter MALVOLIO.

Malvolio. 'Tis but fortune; all is fortune. Maria
once told me she did affect me; and I have heard 21
herself come thus near, that should she fancy, it
should be one of my complexion. Besides, she uses
me with a more exalted respect than any one else
that follows her. What should I think on't?

Sir Toby. Here's an overweening rogue! 26

Fabian. Oh, peace! Contemplation makes a rare 28
turkey-cock of him. How he jets under his advanced
plumes!

Sir Andrew. 'Slight, I could so beat the rogue! 30

Sir Toby. Peace, I say.

Malvolio. To be Count Malvolio! 32

Sir Toby. Ah, rogue!

Sir Andrew. Pistol him, pistol him.

Sir Toby. Peace, peace!

Malvolio. There is example for't; the lady of the
Strachy married the yeoman of the wardrobe.

Sir Andrew. Fie on him, Jezebel! 38

Fabian. O, peace! now he's deeply in. Look how
imagination blows him.

Malvolio. Having been three months married to her,
sitting in my state,—

Sir Toby. Oh, for a stone-bow, to hit him in the eye. 43

Malvolio. Calling my officers about me, in my
branched velvet gown; having come from a day-bed,

1. "Signior": Italian title for a gentle-man (used familiarly by Sir Toby).

2. "scruple": smallest part or iota.

3. "let me be boiled to death with melancholy": almost like saying let me be fried in the refrigerator!

5. "sheep-biter": (Malvolio), dog that worries sheep on the sly.

6. "exult": rejoice.

7. "bear-baiting": form of sport in which dogs worried a bear chained to a post. As a puritan, Malvolio had probably reported Fabian for "bear-baiting" to Olivia, who also disapproved of this cruel sport.

8. "have the bear again": only this time Malvolio will be the bear-victim.

9. "fool him": (until he is) "black and blue" (with anger).

12. "metal of India": gold (priceless wench).

17. "make a contemplative idiot of him": fool him into fantastic imaginings of himself as Olivia's lover and husband.

20. "trout that must be caught with tickling": Malvolio will be caught (trapped) by having his vanity tickled.

21. "affect": like (feel affectionate towards).

26. "overweening": arrogant, presumptuous.

28. "jets": struts.
"advanced plumes": raised feathers (like a turkey-cock's).

30. "'Slight": by God's light (common Elizabethan oath).

32. "Count Malvolio": the steward's imagination is really running away with him; marriage to a countess did not in any case carry with it the gift of the lady's rank in the peerage.

38. "Jezebel": Ahab's shameless wife (1 Kings, xvi et seq.,) Not a very appropriate epithet, but what should one expect from Sir Andrew?

43. "stone-bow": crossbow for throwing stones.

37

TWELFTH NIGHT

ACT II SCENE V

His conjunction with Olivia is so ludicrous that the others can hardly believe their ears. All th's, before he finds the letter! When he finds it, what then?

Seven of his people (in Malvolio's imagination) go and look for Sir Toby because Malvolio has sent for him. Malvolio frowns meanwhile, and perhaps winds up his watch or plays with his chain of office, no—some rich jewel instead.

Toby approaches, curtseys to Malvolio (a delicious steward's dream in which knights curtsey to servants), and listens to Malvolio's ultimatum: either he shall amend his drunkenness, or else he must go. Not only does he drink and carouse excessively, but wastes his time with a foolish knight, one Sir Andrew. Andrew hears from behind the box-hedge, and recognizes himself in the reference to a foolish knight; he has often been called a fool before.

Suddenly Malvolio is jerked back to reality (for a moment) by the sight of a letter lying on the path in front of him. He takes it up. The woodcock is near the trap.

Impelled by curiosity, Malvolio opens this letter and recognizes Olivia's handwriting (as he thinks it is; we know that the letter has been placed there by Maria, who used Olivia's handwriting).

He recognizes certain letters, and mouths them out aloud. Sir Andrew foolishly imitates him behind his back.

---

where I have left Olivia sleeping,—

Sir Toby. Fire and brimstone!

Fabian. Oh, peace, peace!

Malvolio. And then to have the humour of state; and after a demure travel of regard, telling them I know my place as I would they should do theirs, to ask for my kinsman Toby,— 49 50 52

Sir Toby. Bolts and shackles!

Fabian. Oh, peace, peace, peace! now, now.

Malvolio. Seven of my people, with an obedient start, make out for him. I frown the while; and perchance wind up my watch, or play with my—some rich jewel. Toby approaches; courtesies there to me,— 57

Sir Toby. Shall this fellow live?

Fabian. Though our silence be drawn from us with cars, yet peace. 61

Malvolio. I extend my hand to him thus, quenching my familiar smile with an austere regard of control,—

Sir Toby. And does not Toby take you a blow o' the lips then?

Malvolio. Saying, "Cousin Toby, my fortunes having cast me on your niece give me this prerogative of speech,"—

Sir Toby. What, what?

Malvolio. "You must amend your drunkenness."

Sir Toby. Out, scab!

Fabian. Nay, patience, or we break the sinews of our plot.

Malvolio. "Besides, you waste the treasure of your time with a foolish knight,"—

Sir Andrew. That's me, I warrant you.

Malvolio. "One Sir Andrew,"—

Sir Andrew. I knew 'twas I; for many do call me fool.

Malvolio. What employment have we here?

[*Taking up the letter.*

Fabian. Now is the woodcock near the gin. 77

Sir Toby. Oh, peace! and the spirit of humours intimate reading aloud to him! 78

Malvolio. By my life, this is my lady's hand. These be her very C's, her U's, and her T's; and thus makes she her great P's. It is, in contempt of question, her hand. 81 82

Sir Andrew. Her C's, her U's, and her T's. Why that?

Malvolio. [*Reads*] "To the unknown beloved, this, and my good wishes:"—her very phrases! By your leave, wax. Soft! and the impressure her Lucrece, with which she uses to seal. 'Tis my lady. To whom should this be? 86

Fabian. This wins him liver and all.

Malvolio. [*Reads*]

Jove knows I love;
But who?
Lips, do not move;
No man must know.

"No man must know." What follows? the numbers altered. 93

"No man must know"—if this should be thee, Malvolio?

Sir Toby. Marry, hang thee, brock! 96

---

49. "humour of state": dignified personality of the statesman.

50. "demure travel of regard": allowing his eye to travel seriously from one to the other in the room.

52. "kinsman": Sir Toby would have become a relative then.

57. "my . . .": Malvolio was about to say 'my chain' indicating his office as steward, but he recalls that he would not then occupy this lowly place, so quickly changes to 'some rich jewel.'

61. "cars": chariots or carriages (a form of torture in which the victim was torn apart between two such vehicles).

77. "gin": trap (the woodcock was believed to be a rather unintelligent sort of bird).

78. "spirit of humours": in this case the spirit of comedies rather than of elements and proportions.

81. "C": See 89.

82. "P": these two letters do not appear in the letter when Malvolio reads it out, but this inconsistency does not detract from the total dramatic effect of this scene, and few persons would notice it in the audience.

86. "Lucrece": seal engraved with the head of the Roman matron Lucretia, who committed suicide rather than submit to being dishonored.

93. "the numbers altered": the metre changes.

96. "brock": badger or skunk.

TWELFTH NIGHT

ACT II SCENE V

The letter is addressed "To the unknown beloved . . ." and bears a wax seal of Olivia's Lucrece ring. The wax is still soft, so the letter cannot have been sealed long. He asks to whom can this have been addressed, and goes on to read a verse to the effect that no man must know, yet. She may command where she adores, says the second verse. This is a valuable clue, he conjectures. Olivia can command him; he serves her . . .

The writer of the letter says that the letters "M," "O," "A," and "I" do sway her life. This stops him, but only for a moment. Then after a few unheard (by Malvolio, not by us) ejaculations from the box-hedge, he realizes that "M" begins his own name. But the consonants that follow are in the wrong order. That suffers when put to the proof: "A" should follow, but does not. This gives rise to the hope of Sir Toby that he may cudgel Malvolio and make him cry O. "I" comes at the end, Malvolio says.

There immediately follows a retort based upon a play on the letter "I" and the noun "eye." This is obvious, and, at this point, suitable banter.

After the verse there evidently follows what Malvolio nobly calls "prose." It is indeed immortal prose, and involves him deeper still in the plot.

He turns around when told to revolve. Hoots of laughter come from those in the box-hedge, and the audience. He is not to be afraid of greatness. There are three categories of greatness, and Malvolio is about to experience the third: greatness is about to be thrust upon him, he fondly believes. He is to be even more surly with servants, and opposite with Sir Toby. Best of all, he is to dress himself in yellow stockings and is to go in cross-garters. If not, he must remain still a steward and will have demonstrated that he is "not worthy to touch Fortune's fingers." The letter ends endearingly with the pseudonym, "The Fortunate - Unhappy." He takes this to be an oxymoron for Olivia.

Malvolio's mood is exultant after reading this. He invokes daylight and champain, and is evidently in the seventh heaven for a man of his puritanical disposition. He swears to obey all the requests in the letter, and goes over each one conscientiously to make sure that he has not forgotten any of the orders.

Malvolio. [*Reads*]
    I may command where I adore;
      But silence, like a Lucrece knife,
    With bloodless stroke my heart doth gore.
    M, O, A, I, doth sway my life.   100

Fabian. A fustian riddle!   101

Sir Toby. Excellent wench, say I.

Malvolio. "M, O, A, I, doth sway my life." Nay, but first, let me see, let me see, let me see.

Fabian. What dish o' poison has she dressed him?

Sir Toby. And with what wing the staniel checks at it!   106

Malvolio. "I may command where I adore." Why she may command me: I serve her; she is my lady. Why, this is evident to any formal capacity; there is no obstruction in this. And the end,—what should that alphabetical position portend? If I could make that resemble something in me,—Softly! M,O,A,I,—

Sir Toby. Oh, ay, make up that; he is now at a cold scent.

Fabian. Sowter will cry upon't for all this, though it   114
be as rank as a fox.

Malvolio. M,—Malvolio; M,—why, that begins my name.

Fabian. Did not I say he would work it out? the cur is excellent at faults.

Malvolio. M,—but then there is no consonancy in   119
the sequel; that suffers under probation. A should   120
follow, but O does.

Fabian. And O shall end, I hope.

Sir Toby. Ay or I'll cudgel him, and make him cry O!

Malvolio. And then I comes behind.

Fabian. Ay, an you had any eye behind you, you   125
might see more detraction at your heels than fortunes before you.

Malvolio. M, O, A, I. This simulation is not as the   127
former; and yet, to crush this a little, it would bow   128
to me, for every one of these letters are in my name. Soft! here follows prose.

[*Reads*] "If this fall into thy hand, revolve. In my   131
stars I am above thee; but be not afraid of greatness: some are born great, some achieve greatness, and some have greatness thrust upon 'em. Thy fates open their hands; let thy blood and spirit embrace them; and, to inure thyself to what thou art like to be, cast thy humble slough and appear fresh. Be opposite   137
with a kinsman, surly with servants; let thy tongue tang arguments of state; put thyself into the trick of   139
singularity. She thus advises thee that sighs for thee. Remember who commended thy yellow stockings,   140
and wished to see thee ever cross-gartered. I say, remember. Go to, thou art made, if thou desirest to be so; if not, let me see thee a steward still, the   143
fellow of servants, and not worthy to touch Fortune's fingers. Farewell. She that would alter services with thee,

         "The Fortunate-Unhappy."

Daylight and champain discovers not more. This is   146
open. I will be proud, I will read politic authors, I   147
will baffle Sir Toby, I will wash off gross acquaintance, I will be point-devise the very man. I do not   149

---

100. "M,O,A,I,": One critic suggests that these letters may stand for Mare, Orbis, Aer, and Ignis, i.e., Water, Earth, Air, and Fire, the four elements of which the various humors are composed. Another critic suggests that Shakespeare here threw a glance towards the French essayist, MONTAIGNE. Since Maria composed the letter (in theory), may the letters not have differed from MALVOLIO's name just enough to confuse him?

101. "fustian": bombastic, ridiculously pompous (when used as an adjective).

106. "staniel": the hawk is distracted away from the prey by a worthless bird.

114. "Sowter": dog's name, a bungling hound.

119. "no consonancy in the sequel...": a pompous punning way of indicating that the consonants are in the wrong order (consonance, sequence).

120. "suffers under probation": does not stand up to the proof (of observation).
Meanwhile, the actors in the box-hedge make witty and irreverent comments about Malvolio as he seriously tries to figure out the meaning of the letter and its applications to himself.

125. "Ay . . . eye": (and the previously-mentioned letter I): a play upon these words.

127. "simulation": method of representing.

128. "to crush this . . .": with a little straining it would fit me.

131. "revolve": here means consider (but Malvolio literally turns around on stage).

137. "slough": snake skin, garments he wears now.

139. "trick of singularity": mannerisms that make you stand out from the others.

140. "yellow stockings . . .": old-fashioned symbols of jealousy, already laughable.

143. "steward": the actor should stress this word scornfully.

146. "champain": flat open country. "discovers": reveals.

147. "open": the way is clear. "politic": political.

149. "point-devise": to the point of perfection.

TWELFTH NIGHT

ACT II SCENE V

A postscript implores him to smile all the time, "dear my sweet, I prithee." This he will do. In fact, he is prepared to change his own nature, to become, as it were, the positive of his own photographic negative.

Sir Toby says he could marry Maria for having played this trick so well. Actually, he does so, later on in the play.

The comic characters are in excellent spirits when Maria visits them a few seconds later. Toby is prepared to lie under her, her foot upon his neck in the classical position of victor and vanquished, for she has succeeded beyond the hope of possibility.

Sir Andrew feebly apes everything Toby says and does. Toby tells Maria that she has put Malvolio "in such a dream that when the image of it leaves him, he must run mad." Maria has the sense to look forward to the results of this day's work. She tells them to wait until Malvolio first appears before Olivia; he will wear and do everything she detests, and the smiling will be so unsuitable to her melancholy disposition that she will probably have him sent away.

Toby will follow her to the gates of Tartary to see this sight. So will Andrew, of course. They go out arm in arm, a look of eager anticipation in their eyes.

now fool myself, to let imagination jade me; for every reason excites to this, that my lady loves me. She did commend my yellow stockings of late, she did praise my leg being cross-gartered; and in this she manifests herself to my love, and with a kind of injunction drives me to these habits of her liking. I thank my stars I am happy. I will be strange, stout, in yellow stockings, and cross-gartered, even with the swiftness of putting on. Jove and my stars be praised! Here is yet a postscript.

[*Reads*] "Thou canst not choose but know who I am. If thou entertainest my love, let it appear in thy smiling. Thy smiles become thee well; therefore in my presence still smile, dear my sweet, I prithee." Jove, I thank thee. I will smile; I will do everything that thou wilt have me. [*Exit.*

Fabian. I will not give my part of this sport for a pension of thousands to be paid from the Sophy. 167

Sir Toby. I could marry this wench for this device. 168

Sir Andrew. So could I too. 169

Sir Toby. And ask no other dowry with her but such another jest.

Sir Andrew. Nor I neither.

Fabian. Here comes my noble gull-catcher. 173

Re-enter MARIA.

Sir Toby. Wilt thou set thy foot o' my neck? 174

Sir Andrew. Or o' mine either?

Sir Toby. Shall I play my freedom at tray-trip, and become thy bond-slave? 176

Sir Andrew. I' faith, or I either?

Sir Toby. Why, thou hast put him in such a dream, that when the image of it leaves him he must run mad.

Maria. Nay, but say true; does it work upon him?

Sir Toby. Like aqua vitae with a midwife. 182

Maria. If you will then see the fruits of the sport, mark his first approach before my lady. He will come to her in yellow stockings, and 'tis a colour she abhors; and cross-gartered, a fashion she detests; and he will smile upon her, which will now be so unsuitable to her disposition, being addicted to a melancholy as she is, that it cannot but turn him into a notable contempt. If you will see it, follow me. 183 186 189

Sir Toby. To the gates of Tartar, thou most excellent devil of wit! 190

Sir Andrew. I'll make one too. [*Exeunt.*

150 156

150. "jade": deceive or fool.

156. "strange": distant, stand-offish.

167. "Sophy": palace of the Shah of Persia.

168. "marry this wench": Sir Toby Belch does marry Maria towards the end of the play (as is reported in Act V).

169. "So could I too": as usual Andrew's reply is a feeble echo of Toby's vigorous statement.

173. "gull-catcher": Maria (the gull that she has caught being, of course, Malvolio).

174. "set thy foot o' my neck": i.e., act as the victor in a duel and show that she has him at her mercy.

176. "tray-trip": a game played with dice; the object of the game was to throw three consecutive threes.

182. "aqua vitae": literally ardent spirits (high proof alcohol, probably brandy). "midwife": may have been administered to mothers at childbirth by midwives, or else drunk by midwives to relieve the tedium of waiting.

183. "fruits of the sport": results of this trick.

186. "abhors": detests.

189. "notable": because Malvolio is usually calm and sober; noteworthy and notorious.

190. "Tartar": Tartary, or Tartarus, the infernal regions of classical (Greek) mythology, hell. Note how Sir Andrew's answers are all feeble reflections of Sir Toby's replies.

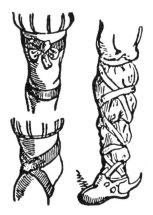

At Olivia's garden, Cesario is chatting with Feste, the jester, who carries a tabor or small drum carried and used by professional clowns and jesters.

They delight in turning one another's sentences inside out, to show their wit. By dallying nicely with words they quickly make them wanton. In this they are being characteristically Elizabethan.

Their wit flows fast and free. Cesario asks the Clown if he is not the lady Olivia's fool, and Feste wittily replies that the lady Olivia has no folly. She will keep no fool until she is married (the implication being that then her fool will be the husband).

Feste says he is not Olivia's fool (i.e., her husband) but her "corrupter of words." Feste also entertains Duke Orsino. Cesario is pleased with Feste's fooling, and gives him a gold coin. "There's expenses for thee."

The Clown prays Jove to send Cesario a beard, noticing his hairless chin. Viola replies that she is almost sick for one; the beard in this case must be understood to be Orsino, but Feste thinks he merely wants to shave to appear grown-up.

While Feste goes in to see if Olivia can see him, Cesario soliloquizes on the nature of playing the fool; to do it well demands a certain measure of intelligence and sensitivity to other people.

ACT THREE, scene one.

(OLIVIA'S GARDEN.)

Enter VIOLA, *and* Clown *with a tabor.*

Viola. Save thee, friend, and thy music. Dost thou live by thy tabor? 2

Clown. No, sir, I live by the church.

Viola. Art thou a churchman?

Clown. No such matter, sir. I do live by the church; 5 for I do live at my house, and my house doth stand by the church.

Viola. So thou mayst say, the king lies by a beggar, if a beggar dwell near him; or, the church stands by thy tabor, if thy tabor stand by the church.

Clown. You have said, sir. To see this age! A sentence is but a cheveril glove to a good wit. How 12 quickly the wrong side may be turned outward!

Viola. Nay, that's certain. They that dally nicely with words may quickly make them wanton. 15

Clown. I would, therefore, my sister had had no name, sir.

Viola. Why, man?

Clown. Why, sir, her name's a word; and to dally with that word might make my sister wanton. But indeed words are very rascals since bonds disgraced them.

Viola. Thy reason, man?

Clown. Troth, sir, I can yield you none without words; and words are grown so false, I am loath to prove reason with them.

Viola. I warrant thou art a merry fellow and carest for nothing.

Clown. Not so, sir, I do care for something; but in my conscience, sir, I do not care for you. If that be to care for nothing, sir, I would it would make you invisible.

Viola. Art not thou the Lady Olivia's fool?

Clown. No, indeed, sir; the Lady Olivia has no folly. She will keep no fool, sir, till she be married; and fools are as like husbands as pilchards are to herrings; the husband's the bigger. I am indeed not her fool, but her corrupter of words. 35

Viola. I saw thee late at the Count Orsino's.

Clown. Foolery, sir, does walk about the orb like 37 the sun, it shines everywhere. I would be sorry, sir, but the fool should be as oft with your master as with my mistress. I think I saw your wisdom there.

Viola. Nay, an thou pass upon me, I'll no more with thee. Hold, there's expenses for thee.

Clown. Now, Jove, in his next commodity of hair, 43 send thee a beard!

Viola. By my troth, I'll tell thee, I am almost sick for one—[*aside*] though I would not have it grow on my chin. Is thy lady within?

Clown. My lady is within, sir. I will construe to 48 them whence you come. Who you are and what you would are out of my welkin, I might say element, 50

---

2. "tabor": small drum used by professional clowns and jesters.

5. all this verbal humor delighted Elizabethan audiences. Do you find it "corny"? Discuss.

12. "cheveril glove": kid leather (easily stretchable).

15. "wanton": not chaste.
The argument is that words are disgraced by being used too freely. Feste delights in setting traps for the unwary; Viola falls into the trap, perhaps voluntarily.

35. "corrupter of words": an excellent definition of Feste's kind of fooling.

37. "orb": poetic word for world.

43. "commodity": quantity of wares, parcel, consignment.

48. "construe": explain (in the scholastic sense).

50. "welkin": sky (= element) used ludicrously by Feste, who claims to be a connoisseur of words, perhaps to parody Cesario, whose own language is choicer than the average messenger's language.

While Cesario is waiting, Sir Toby and Sir Andrew enter. They greet Cesario boisterously but politely, and Sir Andrew parrots some French at him; whereupon he is amazed to receive a reply in French. Cesario does not understand the racing term "taste your legs" and Toby tells him it means to "go on, sir, to enter." Cesario puns on the word gait (gate) but before she can go in, Olivia and Maria come out of the gate. In this sense Cesario is prevented. Shakespeare uses the precise Latin sense of the term.

Cesario uses some poetical expressions to greet Olivia, and Andrew tries to memorize all three for future use. It is clear that Olivia wishes to be alone with Cesario, so she tells them to shut the garden gate and leave her to the hearing in private.

Cesario presents his hand to Olivia, and she graciously asks what his name is. Olivia obviously does not wish to discuss Orsino any further, but if he were to undertake another suit (his own), she would rather hear him "to solicit that/Than music from the spheres." Viola is about to speak when Olivia interrupts to explain the ring episode. She is rather ashamed of sending the ring after Cesario, and wonders what Cesario thinks of her for acting in this way.

but the word is overworn.   [*Exit.*

Viola. This fellow is wise enough to play the fool;
And to do that well craves a kind of wit.
He must observe their mood on whom he jests,
The quality of persons, and the time,
And, like the haggard, check at every feather   62
That comes before his eye. This is a practice
As full of labour as a wise man's art;
For folly that he wisely shows is fit,   65
But wise men, folly-fall'n, quite taint their wit.   66

    Enter SIR TOBY *and* SIR ANDREW.

Sir Toby. Save you, gentlemen.
Viola. And you, sir.
Sir Andrew. Dieu vous garde, monsieur.   69
Viola. Et vous aussi; votre serviteur.
Sir Andrew. I hope, sir, you are; and I am yours.
Sir Toby. Will you encounter the house? my niece   72
is desirous you should enter, if your trade be to her.
Viola. I am bound to your niece, sir; I mean, she is
the list of my voyage.   75
Sir Toby. Taste your legs, sir; put them to motion.   76
Viola. My legs do better understand me, sir, than I
understand what you mean by bidding me taste my   78
legs.
Sir Toby. I mean, to go, sir, to enter.
Viola I will answer you with gait and entrance. But   80
we are prevented. [*Enter Olivia and Maria.*] Most   81
excellent accomplished lady, the heavens rain   82
odours on you!   83
Sir Andrew. That youth's a rare courtier. "Rain
odours," well.
Viola. My matter hath no voice, lady, but to your
own most pregnant and vouchsafed ear.   86
Sir Andrew. "Odours," "pregnant," and "vouch-
    safed."
I'll get 'em all three all ready.
Olivia. Let the garden door be shut, and leave me to
my hearing. [*Exeunt Sir Toby, Sir Andrew, and
Maria.*] Give me your hand, sir.
Viola. My duty, madam, and most humble service.
Olivia. What is your name?
Viola. Cesario is your servant's name, fair princess.
Olivia. My servant, sir! 'Twas never merry world
Since lowly feigning was called compliment.   96
You're servant to the Count Orsino, youth.
Viola. And he is yours, and his must needs be yours.
Your servant's servant is your servant, madam.
Olivia. For him, I think not on him; for his thoughts,
Would they were blanks, rather than fill'd with me!
Viola. Madam, I come to whet your gentle thoughts
On his behalf.
Olivia.   Oh, by your leave, I pray you,
I bade you never speak again of him;
But, would you undertake another suit,   105
I had rather hear you to solicit that
Than music from the spheres.   107
Viola.   Dear lady,—
Olivia. Give me leave, beseech you. I did send,
After the last enchantment you did here,
A ring in chase of you; so did I abuse

62. "haggard": unschooled hawk. "check": swerve aside after. "feather": bird (apart from the true prey).

65. "folly, etc": the folly Feste shows reveals his basic intelligence and wisdom.

66. "But wise men, etc.": but wise men who indulge in folly show themselves to be fundamentally foolish.

69. "Dieu vous garde": the two knights employ French (the language of duelling) out of mocking regard for Cesario.

72. "encounter": affected way of saying go into.

75. "list": aim, purpose.

76. "Taste": test.

77-8. "understand . . . understand": stand under . . . comprehend.

80. "gait": walking (play on gate, entrance).

81. "prevented": the others have arrived before us (Latin for come-before), hence forestalled.

82-3. "rain odours": this is the kind of courtly, conceited language that Toby and Feste and Andrew admire but cannot attain, and therefore mock.

86. "pregnant"; ready. "vouchsafed": offered, ready, attentive.

96. "lowly feigning": sham humility.

105. "suit": wooing on behalf of somebody other than Orsino.

107. "music from the spheres": according to Pythagoras, the universe consisted of eight hollow spheres, inside of which the earth and all the other planets are fixed. The spheres produced a note each which combined to produce perfect harmony which is inaudible to the human ear. The earth is at the center of this system.

TWELFTH NIGHT

ACT III SCENE I

Olivia wants desperately to hear words of love from Cesario, but all Cesario can truthfully say is that he pities her. Olivia says pity is like love, but Cesario says not so, for often we pity our enemies. Olivia behaves with dignity in her disappointment, and relinquishes her claim on the youth; "I will not have you." Yet she says when he does marry, his wife will likely "reap a proper man."

She cannot quite dismiss Cesario before she finds out what he thinks of her.

Now follows an interchange of rapid give and take repartee on the nature of their respective identities. Olivia ends this with a passionate declaration of love for Cesario; she just cannot contain it. "I love thee so, that, maugre all thy pride,/Nor wit nor reason can my passion hide."

Despite this beautiful and spontaneous (and completely unsought) declaration of love, Cesario cannot surrender to Olivia without revealing the disguise; but in refusing her, he is guilty (in her eyes) of wanton cruelty. Nevertheless, he is froced to bid her adieu. Never more will he come again to plead his master's love with Olivia. In desperation, Olivia asks him to come again; you may be able to persuade me to like the man that I now detest. This is a feeble excuse to see Cesario there again.

Myself, my servant, and I fear me, you.
Under your hard construction must I sit,   112
To force that on you, in a shameful cunning,
Which you knew none of yours. What might you
    think?
Have you not set mine honour at the stake
And baited it with all the unmuzzled thoughts
That tyrranous heart can think? To one of your   116
    receiving
Enough is shown. A cypress, not a bosom,   117
Hideth my heart. So, let me hear you speak.
  Viola. I pity you.
  Olivia.   That's a degree to love.
  Viola. No, not a grize; for 'tis a vulgar proof,   121
That very oft we pity enemies.
  Olivia. Why, then, methinks 'tis time to smile again.
O world, how apt the poor are to be proud!
If one should be a prey, how much the better
To fall before the lion than the wolf!   126
                  [*Clock strikes.*
The clock upbraids me with the waste of time.
Be not afraid, good youth, I will not have you;
And yet, when wit and youth is come to harvest,
Your wife is like to reap a proper man.
There lies your way, due west.
  Viola.   Then westward-ho!
Grace and good disposition attend your ladyship!
You'll nothing, madam, to my lord by me?
  Olivia. Stay,
I prithee, tell me what thou think'st of me.
  Viola. That you do think you are not what you are.
  Olivia. If I think so, I think the same of you.
  Viola. Then think you right; I am not what I am.
  Olivia. I would you were as I would have you be!
  Viola. Would it be better, madam, than I am?
I wish it might, for now I am your fool.
  Olivia. Oh, what a deal of scorn looks beautiful
In the contempt and anger of his lip!
A murderous guilt shows not itself more soon
Than love that would seem hid. Love's night is
    noon.
Cesario, by the roses of the spring,
By maidhood, honour, truth and everything,
I love thee so, that, maugre all thy pride,   148
Nor wit nor reason can my passion hide.
Do not extort thy reasons from this clause,   150
For that I woo, thou therefore hast no cause;
But rather reason thus with reason fetter,
Love sought is good, but given unsought is better.
  Viola. By innocence I swear, and by my youth,
I have one heart, one bosom and one truth,
And that no woman has; nor never none
Shall mistress be of it, save I alone.
And so adieu, good madam. Never more   158
Will I my master's tears to you deplore.
  Olivia. Yet come again; for thou perhaps mayest
    move
That heart, which now abhors, to like his love.   161
                  [*Exeunt.*

112. "hard construction": uncharitable interpretation.

116. "receiving": sensitive understanding.

117. "cypress": black gauze used for mourning; Viola can see through this to the love which caused Olivia to descend to these depths.

121. "grize": step, whit.
"vulgar proof": common knowledge.

126. "lion . . . wolf": nobleman . . . servant.
If Olivia sounds bitter, it is only because she is making a great effort to control her feelings.

148. "maugre": despite (Fr. malgre).

150. "Do not extort . . .": do not conclude that because I woo you (against your reason) you have no reason for wooing me . . .

158. "adieu": the final form is used for farewell.
Notice that Olivia has been reduced to the same state as Orsino in this scene. She is pleading for love, and is rejected.

161. Notice that Olivia has been reduced to the same state as Orsino in this scene. She is pleading for love, and is rejected.

ACT III SCENE II

At Olivia's house (downstairs) Sir Andrew is getting fed up because he has made no progress in his attempt to capture the affections of the Countess. That he has failed does not surprise us. She is far too sensitive and intelligent for this foolish knight. They evidently do not move in the same circles. Besides, Andrew is jealous of the favors he has observed Olivia doing the count's serving man, Cesario.

Fabian tries to persuade Andrew that Olivia is only doing favors to Cesario because she wishes to make Andrew jealous: she is really in love with Andrew, says Fabian. The idea is preposterous enough to be believed by Andrew.

Fabian, seeing that Andrew believes this story, now carries it a step further: Andrew should bravely have "banged the youth into dumbness" in front of Olivia, and she would have been so favorably impressed by his courage that she could not fail to love Andrew. His failure to do this means that she has formed an unfavorable opinion of Andrew, that he must now redeem either by some praiseworthy act of bravery or cunning. Andrew says it will have to be by bravery (he is a coward) for he does not possess sufficient skill at cunning. Sir Toby then suggests that Andrew challenge Cecario to fight a duel. Olivia will take note of this. Andrew succumbs to their pressure, and asks if one of them will carry the challenge to Cesario (he is too frightened to deliver it himself).

Toby tells him to write it in a warlike hand, to be curst and brief.

The letter is to be as provoking as possible; he is to employ the intimate "thou" form of address several times, which will be offensive to Cesario. Sir Andrew sets off to do this, and they arrange to meet later at the cubiculo.

Scene two.

(A ROOM IN OLIVIA'S HOUSE.)

Enter SIR TOBY, SIR ANDREW, *and* FABIAN.

Sir Andrew. No, faith, I'll not stay a jot longer. 1
Sir Toby. Thy reason, dear venom, give thy reason. 2
Fabian. You must needs yield your reason, Sir Andrew.
Sir Andrew. Marry, I saw your niece do more favours to the count's serving-man than ever she bestowed upon me. I saw't i' the orchard. 5
Sir Toby. Did she see thee the while, old boy? tell me that.
Sir Andrew. As plain as I see you now.
Fabian. This was a great argument of love in her toward you.
Sir Andrew. Will you make an ass o' me?
Fabian. I will prove it legitimate, sir, upon the oaths of judgment and reason. 13
Sir Toby. And they have been grand-jurymen since 14
before Noah was a sailor.
Fabian. She did show favour to the youth in your sight only to exasperate you, to awake your dormouse valour, to put fire in your heart, and brimstone in your liver. You should then have accosted her; and with some excellent jests, fire-new from the mint, you should have banged the youth into dumbness. This was looked for at your hand, and this was balked. The double gilt of this opportunity you let 23
time wash off, and you are now sailed into the north 24
of my lady's opinion, where you will hang like an icicle on a Dutchman's beard, unless you do redeem it by some laudable attempt either of valour or policy. 27
Sir Andrew. An't be any way, it must be with valour; for policy I hate. I had as lief be a Brownist as a politician. 29
Sir Toby. Why then, build me thy fortunes upon the basis of valour. Challenge me the count's youth to 30
fight with him; hurt him in eleven places. My niece shall take note of it; and assure thyself, there is no love-broker in the world can more prevail in man's 33
commendation with woman than report of valour.
Fabian. There is no way but this, Sir Andrew.
Sir Andrew. Will either of you bear me a challenge to him?
Sir Toby. Go, write it in a martial hand; be curst 38
and brief; it is no matter how witty, so it be eloquent and full of invention. Taunt him with the licence of ink. If thou thou'st him some thrice, it shall not be 40
amiss; and as many lies as will lie in thy sheet of paper, although the sheet were big enough for the bed of Ware in England, set 'em down. Go, about 43
it. Let there be gall enough in thy ink; 44 though thou write with a goose-pen, no matter. About it. 45
Sir Andrew. Where shall I find you?

1-2. Sir Andrew is obviously in a bad mood and makes sniping remarks which is why Sir Toby calls him his 'dear venom.'

5. "count's serving-man"; Cesario.

13. "prove it legitimate": an oath has to fulfill three conditions, truth, judgment, and reason; Fabian deliberately omits the first condition, truth.

14. "grand-jurymen": members of a grand jury, a body that enquired into a case to decide whether it merited going forward to trial.
Sir Andrew's suspicions are lulled, and the others are not likely to lose their source of income for a while at least!

17-18. "dormouse valour": small amount of bravery.

23. "balked": missed.
"double gilt": a doubly golden opportunity.

24. "north, etc": you are now in disfavor with your lady.

27. "policy": scheming and intrigue.

29. "as lief be": as soon be or rather be Brownist, adherent of a sect, the Independents, founded in Elizabeth I's reign by Robert Brown, an English Puritan.

30. The idea of Andrew's challenging Cesario was Sir Toby's invention.

33. "love-broker": go-between in love.

38. "martial": warlike.

40. "if thou thou'st him": thou was a mark of contempt unless the person concerned was a close friend or relative.

43. "bed of Ware": at Ware, in Hertfordshire, there was an oak bedstead big enough to hold twelve adult persons at once.

44. "gall": bitterness or malice; also an ingredient of ink.

45. "goose-pen": the normal quill pen, also held by a 'goose' (Sir Andrew) noted for foolishness and cowardice.

TWELFTH NIGHT

ACT III SCENE II

After he goes out, there is a conversation between Fabian and Sir Toby which begins with a play on the word "dear"; apparently Sir Toby has cost Andrew some two thousand (marks or sovereigns) already. You will recall that Sir Andrew's private income is his chief source of attraction to the others.

Toby is keen on promoting the duel between Sir Andrew and the youthful Cesario, since he anticipates some more fun from this. "Oxen and wainropes cannot hale them together," he believes. Fabian points out that Cesario does not look exactly fierce, and so the matter is arranged.

Maria enters, "the youngest wren of nine" as Sir Toby affectionately calls her, on account of her small size. She is splitting her sides with laughter, for Malvolio ("yond gull") is parading about in yellow stockings! Sir Toby elicits the information that Malvolio is also most villainously cross-gartered! He is obeying every point of the letter, like a pedant, following the text line by line and word by word.

This behavior is likely to prove so obnoxious to the lady Olivia that she will probably strike him, whereat he will probably smile and take the blow as a great favor.

ACT III SCENE III

Walking down a street in the city, not far from the Duke's palace, are Sebastian and Antonio. Sebastian has never been here before, and is an eager sightseer; but Antonio is liable to be arrested on sight if recognized, so why did he risk coming? Because he wanted to be with Sebastian lest any harm come to him, because he likes him so well.

Sir Toby. We'll call thee at the cubiculo. Go.   46
                              [*Exit* SIR ANDREW.

Fabian. This is a dear manakin to you, Sir Toby.   47

Sir Toby. I have been dear to him, lad, some two thousand strong, or so.   48

Fabian. We shall have a rare letter from him; but you'll not deliver't?

Sir Toby. Never trust me, then; and by all means stir on the youth to an answer. I think oxen and wainropes cannot hale them together. For Andrew,   54 if he were opened, and you find so much blood in his liver as will clog the foot of a flea, I'll eat the rest of the anatomy.

Fabian. And his opposite, the youth, bears in his visage no great presage of cruelty.   58

Enter MARIA.

Sir Toby. Look, where the youngest wren of nine   59 comes.

Maria. If you desire the spleen, and will laugh   60 yourselves into stitches, follow me. Yond gull Malvo-   61 lio is turned heathen, a very renegado; for there is   62 no Christian, that means to be saved by believing rightly, can ever believe such impossible passages of grossness. He's in yellow stockings.

Sir Toby. And cross-gartered?

Maria. Most villainously, like a pedant that keeps a   67 school i' the church. I have dogged him, like his murderer. He does obey every point of the letter that I dropped to betray him. He does smile his face into more lines than is in the new map with the augmentation of the Indies; you have not seen such   72 a thing as 'tis. I can hardly forbear hurling things at him. I know my lady will strike him. If she do, he'll smile and take't for a great favour.

Sir Toby. Come, bring us, bring us where he is.

                              [*Exeunt.*

Scene three.

(A STREET.)

Enter SEBASTIAN *and* ANTONIO.

Sebastian. I would not by my will have troubled   1
    you;
But, since you make your pleasure of your pains,
I will no further chide you.   3

Antonio. I could not stay behind you. My desire,
More sharp than filed steel, did spur me forth;
And not all love to see you, though so much   6
As might have drawn one to a longer voyage,
But jealousy what might befall your travel,
Being skilless in these parts, which to a stranger,
Unguided and unfriended, often prove
Rough and unhospitable. My willing love,
The rather by these arguments of fear,
Set forth in your pursuit.

Sebastian.   My kind Antonio,

46. "cubiculo": room, chamber.

47. "manakin": puppet.

48. "dear": expensive.

54. "wainropes": wagon-ropes.

58. "presage": foretelling.

59. "youngest wren of nine": an affectionate allusion to Maria's diminutive stature, based upon the belief that the last hatched of the brood would be the smallest (the wren was also called Our Lady's Hen).

60. "spleen": 'stitches' (from laughter).

61. "gull": 'bird' (he has been gulled, or deceived).

62. "renegado": traitor to his faith.

67. "pedant": schoolmaster.

72. "augmentation of the Indies": the first map of the world (Wright's Mercator projection of 1600) contained more detail of the Indies than previous maps; augmentation means addition to.

1. "by my will": willingly.

3. "chide": rebuke.

6. Antonio has followed Sebastian out of anxiety that Sebastian might encounter some difficulty or danger, being unknown in this country of Illyria.

45

TWELFTH NIGHT

ACT III SCENE III

Sebastian thanks Antonio for taking the risk to come with him, and swears gratitude. He suggests they go see the ancient monuments of the town. The practical seaman says they had better first make sure of their lodgings. This mundane matter does not in the least appeal to Sebastian who is far from tired and anxious to see the sights of the place.

Antonio asks to be excused. He does not without danger of arrest walk the streets, since he was once engaged in battle against the Duke Orsino's sea vessels. This would certainly be remembered and held against him if he were caught.

Antonio hands Sebastian his purse, a singularly generous gesture. They arrange to meet later on at the tavern called The Elephant (the inn called The Elephant and Castle still exists in south London, though it has been rebuilt several times).

Sebastian goes off to see the sights of the town, bearing Antonio's purse, while Antonio makes his way as secretly as possible to the inn. He chose the Elephant because it was away from the busy center of town, and presented less danger of his being recognized.

ACT III SCENE IV

Olivia and Maria are talking in the garden. Olivia has sent to Cesario, and he has promised to come. She is very excited at the prospect and wonders how to treat him, what to give him. She is afraid of seeming to want to buy him. She asks where the sad and civil Malvolio is; he will be a source of comfort to her now.

I can no other answer make but thanks,
And thanks, and ever thanks. Often good turns
Are shuffled off with such uncurrent pay; 16
But, were my worth as is my conscience firm,
You should find better dealing. What's to do?
Shall we go see the reliques of this town? 19
  Antonio. To-morrow, sir. Best first go see your
    lodging.
  Sebastian. I am not weary, and 'tis long to night.
I pray you, let us satisfy our eyes
With the memorials and the things of fame 22
That do renown this city.
  Antonio.   Would you'ld pardon me;
I do not without danger walk these streets. 25
Once, in a sea-fight, 'gainst the count his galleys
I did some service; of such note indeed,
That were I ta'en here it would scarce be answer'd. 28
  Sebastian. Belike you slew great number of his
    people.
  Antonio. The offence is not of such a bloody
    nature;
Albeit the quality of the time and quarrel
Might well have given us bloody argument.
It might have since been answer'd in repaying
What we took from them, which, for traffic's sake, 34
Most of our city did. Only myself stood out;
For which, if I be lapsed in his place, 36
I shall pay dear.
  Sebastian.   Do not then walk to open.
  Antonio. It doth not fit me. Hold, sir, here's my
    purse.
In the south suburbs, at the Elephant, 39
Is best to lodge. I will bespeak our diet, 40
Whiles you beguile the time and feed your knowl-
    edge
With viewing of the town. There shall you have me.
  Sebastian. Why I your purse? 43
  Antonio. Haply your eye shall light upon some toy 44
You have desire to purchase; and your store,
I think, is not for idle markets, sir.
  Sebastian. I'll be your purse-bearer and leave you
For an hour.
  Antonio.   To the Elephant.
  Sebastian. I do remember.   *[Exeunt.*

Scene four.

(OLIVIA'S GARDEN.)

Enter OLIVIA *and* MARIA.

Olivia. I have sent after him; he says he'll come. 1
How shall I feast him? what bestow of him?
For youth is bought more oft than begg'd or 3
    borrow'd.
I speak too loud.
Where is Malvolio? he is sad and civil, 4
And suits well for a servant with my fortunes: 5
Where is Malvolio?

---

16. "shuffled off with such uncurrent pay": brushed off with careless and ungrateful words (if any), or insincere reward.

19. Note the loyalty and friendship between these two men. This is dramatically important when, later Antonio meets Sebastian (as he thinks) again!

22. "memorials": public monuments, major buildings, statues etc.

25. "not without danger": understatement for 'It is very dangerous for me to . . .' (the figure of speech is called LITOTES).

28. "ta'en": taken, captured it would scarce be answered, it (the charge) could scarcely be denied.

34. "traffic's sake": for the sake of trade and commerce.

36. "lapsed": arrested.

39. "the Elephant": the Oliphant Tavern (original of the Elephant and Castle) near the Globe Theater.

40. "bespeak our diet": order our meals.

43. "Why I your purse?": Why do you give me your purse?

44. "toy": trifle that catches your fancy.

1. "him": Cesario.

3. "for youth is bought more oft than begg'd or borrow'd": Olivia is realistic rather than cynical when it comes to purchasing Cesario's affection.

4. "sad and civil": grave and polite.

5. "suits well": fits my own mood.

TWELFTH NIGHT

ACT III SCENE IV

Maria says Malvolio is coming but in a very strange manner; he seems to be mad!

Olivia asks what's the matter with him; "does he rave?" "No," says Maria, "he does nothing but smile." Surely "the man is tainted in's wits!"

Olivia says go and call him here; she feels as mad as Malvolio, if sad and merry madness are equal.

Maria goes out, and returns ushering in Malvolio. The change in the steward is dramatic. Instead of being sad and civil, he smiles broadly and kisses his hand to the lady Olivia. Instead of being dressed in sober black, he is in yellow stockings with tight cross-garters in a contrasting color. Maria hides behind him, her hand over her mouth to prevent great gusts of laughter from escaping.

Malvolio keeps on referring to various lines of the letter he supposes Olivia wrote to him, but since Olivia did not write it, she has no idea what he is talking about. The only one present who does know what he refers to is Maria, and of course she keeps her mouth shut.

He insists on quoting line by line from the letter, and the "greatness" passage comes out again with particular emphasis, much to Olivia's confusion, for she thinks he really is rambling in his mind.

Malvolio runs on, line by line, quoting from the letter, and his quotations are interrupted by startled interjections from Olivia, who thinks this is "very midsummer madness."

The young gentleman from the count is announced, and Olivia and Maria go out to greet him. Before leaving, Olivia says that Malvolio must be looked after; she would not have anything unfortunate happen to him for one half of her dowry. Sir Toby and the others must attend to him.

Maria. He's coming, madam; but in very strange manner. He is, sure, possessed, madam.   8

Olivia. Why, what's the matter? does he rave?

Maria. No, madam, he does nothing but smile. Your ladyship were best to have some guard about   11 you, if he come; for, sure, the man is tainted in's   12 wits.

Olivia. Go call him hither. [*Exit Maria.*] I am as mad as he,
If sad and merry madness equal be.

Re-enter MARIA, *with* MALVOLIO.

How now, Malvolio!

Malvolio. Sweet lady, ho, ho.

Olivia. Smilest thou?
I sent for thee upon a sad occasion.

Malvolio. Sad, lady! I could be sad. This does   18 make some obstruction in the blood, this cross-garter-ing; but what of that? if it please the eye of one, it is with me as the very true sonnet is, "Please one, and please all."

Olivia. Why, how dost thou, man? what is the mat-   23 ter with thee?

Malvolio. Not black in my mind, though yellow in my legs. It did come to his hands, and commands shall be executed. I think we do know the sweet Roman hand.   27

Olivia. God comfort thee! Why dost thou smile so and kiss thy hand so oft?

Maria. How do you, Malvolio?

Malvolio. At your request! yes, nightingales an-   31 swer daws.

Maria. Why appear you with this ridiculous bold-ness before my lady?

Malvolio. "Be not afraid of greatness." 'Twas well writ.   36

Olivia. What meanest thou by that, Malvolio?

Malvolio. "Some are born great,"—

Olivia. Ha!

Malvolio. "Some achieve greatness,"—

Olivia. What sayest thou?

Malvolio. "And some have greatness thrust upon them."

Olivia. Heaven restore thee!

Malvolio. "Remember who commended thy yellow stockings,"—

Olivia. Thy yellow stockings!

Malvolio. "And wished to see thee cross-gartered."

Olivia. Cross-gartered!

Malvolio. "Go to, thou art made, if thou desirest to   48 be so;"—

Olivia. Am I made?

Malvolio. "If not, let me see thee a servant still."

Olivia. Why, this is very midsummer madness.

Enter Servant.

Servant. Madam, the young gentleman of the Count Orsino's is returned. I could hardly entreat him back. He attends your ladyship's pleasure.

Olivia. I'll come to him. [*Exit Servant.*] Good Maria, let this fellow be looked to. Where's my cousin Toby? Let some of my people have a special care of

8. "possessed": out of his mind (which has been taken over by the devil).

11. "guard": to protect her (reference to the ancient belief that all madmen are violent and refractory).

12. "tainted in's wits": of a diseased mind.

18. This is Malvolio's most striking entrance, one for which we and he are prepared.

23. Olivia is scared. Can this be her sober-suited steward?

27. "Roman hand": the Italian style of handwriting which was becoming fashionable during the sixteenth century; it resembled printer's italic.

31. Malvolio tells Olivia he is obeying her request (a reference to the letter which, of course, the countess knows nothing about). Then he turns scornfully to Maria, and compares himself to a poetic nightingale answering her, a common crow or jack-daw!

36. The repetition of key phrases and sentences from the letter is dramatically ironic, for Maria knows what he is saying, but pretends not to know; Olivia does not know, and believes her steward is indeed mad; while the audience knows, sees the mistake, and laughs.

48. "made": a play on 'thy fortune's made,' maid, and mad.
Olivia does not realize that Malvolio is quoting; she assumes his talk to be the raving of a madman, and she wishes that he would go to bed and be treated.
Maria cunningly asks Malvolio questions that cause him to go quoting from the letter, to heighten the impression of raving.

47

TWELFTH NIGHT

ACT III SCENE IV

If Olivia's mind is set on marriage, the reference to one half of her dowry is misleading, for it confirms Malvolio in the belief that Olivia is contemplating marrying him. This confirmation (as he supposes) leads him to behave in a very scornful and arrogant manner towards Sir Toby and Fabian when they come in with Maria to attend to him a few moments later.

He thinks Olivia wanted to be familiar when she referred to him as "fellow." He believes that she is in love with him and will entertain no evidence to the contrary.

Toby and Fabian come in, looking as though they are prepared to pacify a raving lunatic. It was the custom at this time to treat the insane worse than criminals, and they were often restrained by force (not gently either) and thrown into prison, usually solitary confinement. Toby and Fabian roughly seize hold of Malvolio's arms and almost knock him over with the force of their clasp.

He tries to discard them, but they cling like limpets. There is quite a lot of jostling, and poor Malvolio (we begin to feel sorry for him at this point in the play for the first time) is given quite a rough time.

There are various references to being possessed by the devil, an ancient superstition that was current at this time.

Fabian says there is no way to handle him but with gentleness, and they proceed to virtually beat him up. This action should be highly exaggerated on stage, and Malvolio should be indignant and outraged.

him. I would not have him miscarry for the half of my dowry.   [*Exeunt* OLIVIA *and* MARIA.

Malvolio. Oho! do you come near me now? no worse man than Sir Toby to look to me! This concurs directly with the letter: she sends him on purpose, that I may appear stubborn to him; for she incites me to that in the letter. "Cast thy humble slough," says she; "be opposite with a kinsman, surly with servants; let thy tongue tang with arguments of state; put thyself into the trick of singularity;" and consequently sets down the manner how: as, a sad face, a reverend carriage, a slow tongue, in the habit of some sir of note, and so forth. I have limed her; but it is Jove's doing, and Jove make me thankful! And when she went away now, "Let this fellow be looked to." "Fellow!" not Malvolio, nor after my degree, but "fellow." Why, everything adheres together, that no dram of a scruple, no scruple of a scruple, 73 no obstacle, no incredulous or unsafe circumstance— 74 What can be said? Nothing that can be can come between me and the full prospect of my hopes. Well, Jove, not I, is the doer of this, and he is to be thanked.

Re-enter MARIA, *with* SIR TOBY *and* FABIAN.

Sir Toby. Which way is he, in the name of sanctity? 78 If all the devils of hell be drawn in little, and Legion 79 himself possessed him, yet I'll speak to him.

Fabian. Here he is, here he is. How is't with you, sir? how is't with you, man?

Malvolio. Go off; I discard you. Let me enjoy my private. Go off.   84

Maria. Lo, how hollow the fiend speaks within him! 85 did not I tell you? Sir Toby, my lady prays you to have a care of him.

Malvolio. Aha! does she so?

Sir Toby. Go to, go to; peace, peace; we must deal gently with him. Let me alone. How do you, Malvolio? how is't with you? What, man! defy the devil. Consider, he's an enemy to mankind.

Malvolio. Do you know what you say?

Maria. La you, an you speak ill of the devil, how he 94 takes it at heart! Pray God, he be not bewitched! My lady would not lose him for more than I'll say.

Malvolio. How now, mistress!

Maria. O Lord!

Sir Toby. Prithee, hold thy peace; this is not the way. Do you not see you move him? let me alone with him.

Fabian. No way but gentleness; gently, gently. The fiend is rough, and will not be roughly used.

Sir Toby. Why, how now, my bawcock! how dost thou, chuck?   106

Malvolio. Sir!

Sir Toby. Ay, Biddy, come with me. What, man! 108 'tis not for gravity to play at cherry-pit with Satan. Hang him, foul collier!   110

Maria. Get him to say his prayers, good Sir Toby, get him to pray.

Malvolio. My prayers, minx!

73. "dram": small amount.
   "scruple": third of a dram or small quantity.

74. "incredulous": incredible.

78. in the name of sanctity, in dealing with devils (supposed) Sir Toby invokes the name of holiness.

79. "Legion": allusion to the man possessed of many devils in the country of the Gadarenes; refer to Mark, v, 9 and Luke, viii, 30.

84. "private": privacy.

85. "fiend": devil.

94. "speak ill of the devil": Maria turns all Malvolio's replies into evidence of his disordered mind.

106. "bawcock": fine fellow (at this point, Sir Toby might slap Malvolio on the shoulder, almost knocking him down, as an example of the 'gentleness' with which they treat the devil that possesses him; a fine revenge!

108. "Biddy": common name for a hen (very insulting to Malvolio).

110. "foul collier": coal-miner (black, like the devil).

ACT III SCENE IV

They let him go, and he stalks off, much hurt in dignity but with his belief in himself and his lady's love unimpaired.

Toby has the idea of having Malvolio shut up in a dark room, as was customary for lunatics in those days. This idea appeals to all the others concerned, and they hasten to execute the plan.

Sir Andrew enters, and Fabian says somewhat ironically that here comes "more matter for a May morning." Andrew is proud of the challenge he has prepared for Cesario, but in fact it is a ridiculous piece of writing. It is also highly irrelevant (on its own showing). Toby reads it aloud, and it is indeed a comic enough challenge.

Andrew is very buoyed-up by the challenge he has written. Maria informs him that Cesario is now having a conversation with Olivia, and Sir Toby tells Andrew to go and wait for Cesario at every street corner and to deliver the challenge with drawn sword, swearing horribly. This will so frighten Cesario that he will be terrified to fight the duel.

Andrew goes off to carry out these instructions, and then Sir Toby reveals that he does not intend to deliver the foolish written challenge: instead, he will deliver the challenge by word of mouth, so that Cesario will not know that it comes from a clodpole like Sir Andrew.

Sir Toby intends to terrify Cesario, by exaggerating Andrew's bravery, rage, skill, fury, and impetuosity; he knows that when it comes to the test Andrew will also be terrified: "they will kill one another by the look, like cockatrices."

Toby and the other two in the subplot exeunt, the former meditating upon some horrid message for a challenge; meanwhile, in another part of the countess' garden, Olivia and Cesario continue a conversation that is, by its very nature, at cross-purposes since they are both of the same sex. Olivia thinks Cesario has a heart of stone; the opposite is the case, as we know but she does not (dramatic irony).

Olivia gives Cesario a bejeweled brooch containing a portrait of the countess inside it; she sends a message of no comfort to the Duke Orsino, but pleads with the messenger to come again tomorrow.

Maria. No, I warrant you, he will not hear of godliness.

Malvolio. Go, hang yourselves all! you are idle shallow things; I am not of your element. You shall 115 know more hereafter. 　　　　　　　　　　[*Exit.*

Sir Toby. Is't possible?

Fabian. If this were played upon a stage now, I could condemn it as an improbable fiction.

Sir Toby. His very genius hath taken the infection 120 of the device, man.

Maria. Nay, pursue him now, lest the device take 123 air and taint.

Fabian. Why, we shall make him mad indeed.

Maria. The house will be the quieter.

Sir Toby. Come, we'll have him in a dark room and bound. My niece is already in the belief that he's mad. We may carry it thus, for our pleasure and his penance, till our very pastime, tired out of breath, prompt us to have mercy on him, at which time we will bring the device to the bar and crown thee for 132 a finder of madmen. But see, but see!

Enter SIR ANDREW.

Fabian. More matter for a May morning.

Sir Andrew. Here's the challenge, read it. I warrant there's vinegar and pepper in't. 　　　　　　136

Fabian. Is't so saucy? 　　　　　　　　　　137

Sir Andrew. Ay, is't, I warrant him. Do but read.

Sir Toby. Give me. [*Reads*] "Youth, whatsoever thou art, thou art but a scurvy fellow."

Fabian. Good, and valiant.

Sir Toby. [*Reads*] "Wonder not, nor admire not in thy mind, why I do call thee so, for I will show thee no reason for't."

Fabian. A good note; that keeps you from the blow 144 of the law. 　　　　　　　　　　　　　145

Sir Toby. [*Reads*] "Thou comest to the lady Olivia, and in my sight she uses thee kindly; but thou liest in thy throat. That is not the matter I challenge thee for." 　　　　　　　　　　148

Fabian. Very brief, and to exceeding good sense—less. 149

Sir Toby. [*Reads*] "I will waylay thee going home, where if it be thy chance to kill me"—

Fabian. Good.

Sir Toby. [*Reads*] "Thou killest me like a rogue and a villain."

Fabian. Still you keep o' the windy side of the law; 153 good.

Sir Toby. [*Reads*] "Fare thee well; and God have mercy upon one of our souls! He may have mercy upon mine; but my hope is better, and so look to thyself. Thy friend, as thou usest him, and thy sworn enemy, ANDREW AGUECHEEK." If this letter move him not, his legs cannot. I'll give it him.

Maria. You may have very fit occasion for't; he is now in some commerce with my lady, and will by 163 and by depart.

Sir Toby. Go, Sir Andrew; scout me for him at the corner of the orchard like a bum-baily. So soon as 164 ever thou seest him, draw; and, as thou drawest, 165 swear horrible; for it comes to pass oft that a terrible

115. "element": class.

120. his innermost nature has caused him to fall for the trick.

123-4. "take air and taint": become known and spoil.

132. "bring the device to the bar": bring the trick out into the open, to be judged (a flavor of the law is in these words).

136-7. saucy fits in with the references to vinegar and pepper previously mentioned.

144-5. "keeps you from the blow of the law": is not actionable in the law courts.

148. The irrelevancy diminishes the force of this challenge, and renders it ridiculous.

149. "sense—less": the last word is spoken as an aside to the audience; it is not for Andrew's ears.

153. "windy side of the law": windward (protected) side.

163. "commerce": business.

164. "bum-baily": sheriff's officer of inferior rank who lay in wait to arrest debtors.

165. "drawest": (thy sword).

As they go out, Sir Toby and Fabian re-enter. On seeing Cesario, they go up to him (her) and Sir Toby tells him that his "interceptor" (Sir Andrew) awaits him in the orchard. He is Cesario's assailant, and is quick, skillful, and deadly.

Taken by surprise, this is too much for Viola. She is sure Sir Toby has made a mistake. She has done offense to nobody.

Toby assures her that there is no mistake. She had better take care, for her opponent is youthful, strong, skillful, and angry. He is a knight, knighted in the drawing room rather than on the battlefield, yet he is a devil in private brawl. He has killed three men in previous duels, and he is currently

oath, with a swaggering accent sharply twanged off, gives manhood more approbation than ever proof itself would have earned him. Away!

Sir Andrew. Nay, let me alone for swearing. [*Exit.*

Sir Toby. Now will not I deliver his letter: for the behaviour of the young gentleman gives him out to be of good capacity and breeding; his employment between his lord and my niece confirms no less. Therefore this letter, being so excellently ignorant, will breed no terror in the youth. He will find it comes from a clodpole. But, sir, I will deliver his 177 challenge by word of mouth; set upon Aguecheek a notable report of valour; and drive the gentleman, as I know his youth will aptly receive it, into a most hideous opinion of his rage, skill, fury and impetuosity. This will so fright them both that they will kill one another by the look, like cockatrices. 182

Re-enter OLIVIA, *with* VIOLA.

Fabian. Here he comes with your niece; give them way till he take leave, and presently after him. 184

Sir Toby. I will meditate the while upon some horrid 185 message for a challenge.

[*Exeunt* SIR TOBY, FABIAN, *and* MARIA.

Olivia. I have said too much unto a heart of stone
And laid mine honour too unchary out. 188
There's something in me that reproves my fault;
But such a headstrong potent fault it is,
That it but mocks reproof.

Viola. With the same 'haviour that your passion 192
bears
Goes on my master's grief.

Olivia. Here, wear this jewel for me, 'tis my picture. 195
Refuse it not; it hath no tongue to vex you;
And I beseech you come again to-morrow.
What shall you ask of me that I'll deny,
That honour saved may upon asking give?

Viola. Nothing but this, your true love for my
master.

Olivia. How with mine honour may I give him that
Which I have given to you?

Viola.   I will acquit you.

Olivia. Well, come again to-morrow. Fare the well.
[*Exit.*

Re-enter SIR TOBY *and* FABIAN.

Sir Toby. Gentlemen, God save thee.

Viola. And you, sir.

Sir Toby. That defence thou hast, betake thee to 't. Of what nature the wrongs are thou hast done him, I 207 know not; but thy interceptor, full of despite, bloody as the hunter, attends thee at the orchard-end. Dismount thy tuck, be yare in the preparation, for thy 210 assailant is quick, skilful, and deadly. 211

Viola. You mistake, sir; I am sure no man hath any quarrel to me. My remembrance is very free and clear from any image of offence done to any man.

Sir Toby. You'll find it otherwise, I assure you. Therefore, if you hold your life at any price, betake you to your guard; for your opposite hath in him what youth, strength, skill, and wrath can furnish man withal.

177. "clodpole": blockhead.
182. "cockatrices": mythological creatures, half serpent, half cockerel, famed for killing at a glance.

184. "presently": immediately (in the present) (the modern idea of delay is not here).

185. "horrid": terrifying.

188. "too unchary out": thriftlessly squandered my good name.

192. "'haviour": behavior, conduct.

195. "jewel": diamond brooch containing a miniature portrait of Olivia (Viola probably wants to refuse this gift, but does not do so for fear of offending the countess even further).

207. "him": Sir Andrew Aguecheek, Cesario's 'interceptor' or challenger.

210. "Dismount thy tuck": take thy rapier out of its scabbard or sheath.
"be yare in thy preparation": be ready (hence, nimble, brisk) in getting ready for this duel.

211. "thy assailant": Sir Andrew Aguecheek quick, skilful, and deadly,—but only in Sir Toby's imagination!

TWELFTH NIGHT

ACT III SCENE IV

so angry that only the death, and burial, of his opponent can placate him.

Cesario's impulse is to return to Olivia's house to beg the protection of the countess. Perhaps this Sir Andrew is one of those men she has heard about, who provoke quarrels deliberately on others to find out if they are courageous or not. No, he is not like that, says Sir Toby; he is suffering from a very real injury that you have done him, and therefore you should "strip your sword stark naked."

Not surprisingly, Viola finds these proceedings "as uncivil as strange" and she implores Sir Toby to send to the knight to find out what her offense to him is. It must be a deed of omission rather than one of commission.

Toby exits, pretending to go and find out what it is that Andrew is offended about, leaving Cesario to the tender mercies of Signior (the title is new, for the occasion) Fabian.

Fabian grabs Cesario by the arm, and tries to make him walk in the direction of Sir Andrew, meanwhile telling Cesario of Andrew's bloody and fatal skill in dueling. He promises to make Cesario's peace with him if he can, and Viola thanks him for doing this.

As they go out one side of the stage, Sir Toby enters grabbing Sir Andrew by the arm from another entrance. Andrew is reluctant to go on, and Toby tells him that Cesario is the very devil: he strikes with his sword in such a manner that it (a casual reference to death) is inevitable. Andrew quakes. They say that Cesario learned how to fence so well, that he taught the art at the Sophy. Andrew quails.

Andrew says he'll not meddle with Cesario. Toby pushes and prods him onward. The fact that Cesario teaches fencing (according to the legend built up by Toby) impresses Andrew so much that he promises to give Cesario his horse, gray Capilet, if he will agree to let the matter slip.

Toby stops at this, and says he will try it out and see if he can negotiate the peace. He hopes to keep the horse for himself.

Viola. I pray you, sir, what is he?

Sir Toby. He is knight, dubbed with unhatched 220 rapier and on carpet consideration; but he is a 221 devil in private brawl. Souls and bodies hath he divorced three; and his incensement at this mo- 223 ment is so implacable, that satisfaction can be none but by pangs of death and sepulchre. Hob, nob, is 224 his word; give't or take't.

Viola. I will return again into the house and desire some conduct of the lady. I am no fighter. I have 227 heard of some kind of men that put quarrels pur- posely on others, to taste their valour. Belike this is a man of that quirk. 229

Sir Toby. Sir, no; his indignation derives itself out of a very competent injury. Therefore, get you 231 on and give him his desire. Back you shall not to the house, unless you undertake that with me which with as much safety you might answer him. There- fore, on, or strip your sword stark naked; for meddle you must, that's certain, or forswear to wear 236 iron about you.

Viola. This is as uncivil as strange. I beseech you, do me this courteous office, as to know of the knight what my offence to him is. It is something of my negligence, nothing of my purpose.

Sir Toby. I will do so. Signior Fabian, stay you by this gentleman till my return. [*Exit.*

Viola. Pray you, sir, do you know of this matter?

Fabian. I know the knight is incensed against you, even to a mortal arbitrement; but nothing of the 245 circumstance more.

Viola. I beseech you, what manner of man is he?

Fabian. Nothing of that wonderful promise, to read him by his form, as you are like to find him in the proof of his valour. He is, indeed, sir, the most skil- ful, bloody, and fatal opposite that you could pos- sibly have found in any part of Illyria. Will you walk towards him? I will make your peace with him if I can.

Viola. I shall be much bound to you for't. I am one that had rather go with sir priest than sir knight. I 255 care not who knows so much of my mettle.

[*Exeunt.*

Re-enter SIR TOBY, *with* SIR ANDREW.

Sir Toby. Why, man, he's a very devil; I have not seen such a firago. I had a pass with him, rapier, 257 scabbard and all, and he gives me the stuck in with such a mortal motion, that it is inevitable; and on the answer, he pays you as surely as your feet hit the ground they step on. They say he has been fencer to the Sophy. 262

Sir Andrew. I'll not meddle with him. 263

Sir Toby. Ay, but he will not now be pacified. 264 Fabian can scarce hold him yonder.

Sir Andrew. Plague on't, an' I thought he had been valiant and so cunning in fence, I'ld not have 267 challenged him. Let him let the matter slip, and I'll give him my horse, gray Capilet. 269

Sir Toby. I'll make the motion. Stand here, make a 270 good show on't; this shall end without the perdition 272

220-1. "dubbed with unhatched rapier": knighted with his own sword that had not been hacked in battle.

221. "carpet consideration": while kneeling, not on the field of battle, but on a carpet.

223. "incensement": anger.

224. "Hob, nob": hit or miss.

227. "conduct": safe conduct.

229. "quirk": odd behavior.

231. "competent injury": legitimate and substantial wrong.

236. "wear iron": wear a sword.

245. "mortal arbitrament": settle a dis- pute by duelling to the death of one contestant.

255. "sir priest": common title for priests. (refer to Sir Topas the curate).

257. "firago": virago (heroic maiden) For a similar play on words refer to Humbert Wolfe's definition of a chaste female cabinet-minister as a 'virago intacta.'

262. "fencer to the Sophy": taught fenc- ing to the Shah of Persia.

263. "I'll not meddle with him": Sir An- drew's cowardly disposition becomes evident.

264. "but he will not now be pacified": it is clear that Sir Toby is the insti- gator of this duel since neither of the antagonists wishes to meddle with the other.

267. "in fence": in the art of fencing.

269. "gray Capilet": the name of the horse with which Sir Andrew wished to bribe Viola not to fight.

270. "I'll make the motion": to act as though doing something; nowadays means to do something so casually that one does it at all.

272. "perdition": loss.

TWELFTH NIGHT

ACT III SCENE IV

At this point Fabian and Viola re-enter. Fabian and Toby meet, as seconds, in the center, while the two reluctant opponents, each in dread of the other, confront one another woefully from opposite ends of the stage.

Toby returns to his champion, Cesario, and says there is no remedy: there has to be a duel. Andrew has forgotten what they are to fight about, but he has sworn to fight, so fight he must, for the sake of the oath. Cesario hopes his doublet is not cut or torn by the other's sword, else her female characteristics will soon be revealed.

With Fabian pushing on Cesario, and Toby pushing on Andrew, they finally meet and tremulously take out their swords. Each fears for his life, and the audience loves it.

As they meet, sword timorously pointed at sword, there is a sudden, dramatic interruption: a true and vigorous swordsman intervenes. It is Antonio; he tells them to put up their swords, and goes over to the defense of Cesario. He evidently mistakes Cesario for the twin-brother, Sebastian. Unaware of the error, he says that if this young gentleman has done offense, he will take the blame for it.

Toby is annoyed to have his sport spoiled at this point, and he draws his own weapon and starts to fight with Antonio. Antonio easily beats him, and would have done more damage to Toby than he did if the officers of the guard had not entered and seized him. Antonio is now a prisoner.

Toby goes off, bleeding; Fabian runs away from the officers, smelling trouble. Antonio is arrested, and Andrew and Viola are left together to settle their own differences without further recourse to arms. Andrew offers Cesario the horse (gray Capilet). Cesario, of course, has no idea what Andrew is talking about, since Toby did not divulge this generous offer to him.

of souls. [*Aside.*] Marry, I'll ride your horse as well as I ride you.

Re-enter FABIAN *and* VIOLA.

[*To Fabian.*] I have his horse to take up the quar- 273 rel; I have persuaded him the youth's a devil.

Fabian. He is as horribly conceited of him; and pants and looks pale, as if a bear were at his heels.

Sir Toby. [*To Viola*] There's no remedy, sir; he will fight with you for oath's sake. Marry, he hath better bethought him of his quarrel, and he finds that now scarce to be worth talking of; therefore draw, for the supportance of his vow. He protests 281 he will not hurt you.

Viola. [*Aside.*] Pray God defend me! A little thing 282 would make me tell them how much I lack of a man.

Fabian. Give ground, if you see him furious.

Sir Toby. Come, Sir Andrew, there's no remedy; the gentleman will, for his honour's sake, have one bout with you; he cannot by the duello avoid it. But 287 he has promised me, as he is a gentleman and a sol-dier, he will not hurt you. Come on; to't.

Sir Andrew. Pray God, he keep his oath!

Viola. I do assure you, 'tis against my will. 290

[*They draw.*

Enter ANTONIO.

Antonio. Put up your sword. If this young gentle-man
Have done offence, I take the fault on me.
If you offend him, I for him defy you.

Sir Toby. You, sir! why, what are you?

Antonio. One, sir, that for his love dares yet do more
Than you have heard him brag to you he will.

Sir Toby. Nay, if you be an undertaker, I am for you. 298

[*They draw.*

Enter Officers.

Fabian. O good Sir Toby, hold! here come the officers.

Sir Toby. [*To Antonio.*] I'll be with you anon. 300

Viola. Pray, sir, put your sword up, if you please.

Sir Andrew. Marry, will I, sir; and for that I prom-ised you, I'll be as good as my word. He will bear 304 you easily and reins well.

First Officer. This is the man; do thy office. 306

Second Officer. Antonio, I arrest thee at the suit 307 of Count Orsino.

Antonio. You do mistake me, sir.

First Officer. No, sir, no jot; I know your favour 309 well,
Though now you have no sea-cap on your head.
Take him away; he knows I know him well.

Antonio. I must obey. [*To Viola.*] This comes with
seeking you:
But there's no remedy; I shall answer it.
What will you do, now my necessity
Makes me to ask you for my purse? It grieves me 315
Much more for what I cannot do for you
Than what befalls myself. You stand amazed;
But be of comfort.

273. The two seconds, Sir Toby and Fa-bian meet in the center, and ex-change confidential words; they then return to their masters.

281. "supportance of his vow": in order not to break his oath.

282. "A little thing": a small rip of the doublet by the opponent's sword would soon reveal the fact that Viola is a woman.

287. "the duello": the strict rules of duel-ling.

290. They draw. Thus commences one of the most ludicrous duels in stage his-tory, no sooner begun than ended by the intervention of Antonio.

298. "undertaker": one who is spoiling for a fight.
A second duel begins, between Sir Toby Belch and Antonio, but this, too, is stopped, by the intervention of Orsino's officers who have come to arrest Antonio (who has been recognized).

300. Sir Toby flees.

304-5. "He will bear you easily and reins well": Sir Andrew here gives Sir Toby the horse, gray Capilet.

306. "office": duty.

307. "suit": on behalf of.

309. "no jot": not an iota (a little, a point).

315. "... to ask you for my purse": An-tonio mistakes Viola for Sebastian, and is shaken and dumb-founded to meet a refusal.

TWELFTH NIGHT

ACT III SCENE IV

The officers tell Antonio that he has been recognized as a member of a rival sea-force that once fought against Duke Orsino's ships and wrought considerable damage upon them. Antonio turns to Viola (mistakenly taken for Sebastian) and says that this is what comes of looking for his friend. There's nothing for it; I shall have to go with them. May I please have the purse of money I gave you previously before you went off on this pleasure-spree?

What purse? Viola wonders what on earth this strange man is talking about. The second officer tells Antonio he must come away, and Antonio is desperate: he must have his money back to purchase a proper defense.

He cannot at all understand why his so-called friend, Sebastian, is being so obstinate and stupid at this time.

Viola understands that the strange man needs money, and gives him half of his own coffer. Antonio does not want a gift; he wants his own money returned. Will you deny me in the hour of need, he calls, and the officers drag him off. As he goes, he recounts how he saved that youth's life in the shipwreck, and this is how he is repaid.

The officers are not interested in the tale that their prisoner is telling as they drag him off. Somebody called Sebastian has let him down badly, and Antonio is naive enough to have believed in this man, whoever Sebastian is. Antonio is so overcome by the perfidiousness of this ingratitude that he almost starts raving. The officers think he is going mad. They take him out.

On stage, after all this turmoil, is Cesario; she has been listening to Antonio, and has partly guessed what happened. The Sebastian rescued from the waves by Antonio may turn out to be her own brother. If so, she has now been mistaken for him. How wonderful if this turns out to be the case!

Toby and Fabian are in a chastened mood, and go off together to whisper about serious things. Toby has been wounded.

Viola goes on thinking about this encounter with Antonio; he named Sebastian, and it may be her brother is still alive and on this very sea-shore.

She is very excited by the prospect of meeting her brother, presumed drowned, once more.

Second Officer. Come, sir, away.

Antonio. I must entreat of you some of that money.

Viola. What money, sir? 321
For the fair kindness you have show'd me here,
And, part, being prompted by your present trouble,
Out of my lean and low ability
I'll lend you something. My having is not much;
I'll make division of my present with you. 326
Hold, there's half my coffer. 327

Antonio. Will you deny me now?
Is't possible that my deserts to you
Can lack persuasion? Do not tempt my misery,
Lest that it make me so unsound a man
As to upbraid you with those kindnesses
That I have done for you.

Viola. I know of none;
Nor know I you by voice or any feature.
I hate ingratitude more in a man
Than lying vainness, babbling drunkenness,
Or any taint of vice whose strong corruption
Inhabits our frail blood.

Antonio. O heavens themselves!

Second Officer. Come, sir, I pray you, go.

Antonio. Let me speak a little. This youth that you
  see here
I snatch'd one half out of the jaws of death,
Relieved him with such sanctity of love, 341
And to his image, which methought did promise
Most venerable worth, did I devotion.

First Officer. What's that to us? The time goes by;
  away!

Antonio. But oh, how vile an idol proves this god! 345
Thou hast, Sebastian, done good feature shame.
In nature there's no blemish but the mind; 347
None can be called deform'd but the unkind;
Virtue is beauty, but the beauteous-evil
Are empty trunks o'erflourish'd by the devil.

First Officer. The man grows mad; away with
  him!
Come, come, sir.

Antonio. Lead me on. [*Exit with Officers.*

Viola. Methinks his words do from such passion
  fly,
That he believes himself. So do not I.
Prove true, imagination, O prove true,
That I, dear brother, be now ta'en for you! 356

Sir Toby. Come hither, knight; come hither,
Fabian; we'll whisper o'er a couplet or two of most
sage saws. 358

Viola. He named Sebastian. I my brother know
Yet living in my glass; even such and so
In favour was my brother, and he went
Still in this fashion, colour, ornament,
For him I imitate. Oh, if it prove,
Tempests are kind and salt waves fresh in love. 364
  [*Exit.*

Sir Toby. A very dishonest paltry boy, and more a
coward than a hare. His dishonesty appears in
leaving his friend here in necessity and denying
him; and for his cowardship, ask Fabian.

321. "What money, sir?": Viola wonders what this man is talking about, but seeing his necessity, graciously consents to lend him some of the small amount of money she has herself. This seems gross ingratitude to Antonio, who believes that Sebastian is denying ever having been acquainted with him.

326. "present": current holdings.

327. "coffer": chest, treasury, bank.

341. "sanctity of love": the friendship that is holy.

345. "this god": Sebastian is god-like to the simple-hearted Antonio.

347. In the world of nature there is no fault save what exists in men's minds.

356. Viola hopes that she may indeed have been mistaken for her brother, Sebastian, for this may mean that her brother is still alive.

358. "saws": maxims, aphorisms.

364. "Tempests are kind": storms produce good results as well as tragic ones.

TWELFTH NIGHT

ACT III SCENE IV

Sir Toby thinks Cesario is very dishonest to steal a purse and deny a friend; and Fabian can prove he did not want to fight Andrew, so he is a coward as well. Andrew recovers some of his own brave spirits (they had evaporated) and says that he'll go after him (Cesario) again and beat him this time. Toby says, yes, "cuff him soundly, but never draw thy sword." They follow to watch the event. We wonder what is going to happen if Andrew catches, not Cesario, but Sebastian.

ACT IV SCENE I

In the street before Countess Olivia's house, the Clown, Feste, has been sent by Olivia to Cesario; when he sees Sebastian, he naturally mistakes him for Cesario (the two were twins) and, of course, Sebastian does not know what the Clown is talking about! They are at cross-purposes, and the audience (but not the characters) knows why. This is dramatic irony used to produce a comic effect, and the situation is hilarious. This is also called situational comedy, or humor of situation.

Sebastian pays the Clown to go, for he is proving tiresome; this contrasts to the amusement that Cesario found in the Clown previously. Feste disappears, and Sir Andrew, Sir Toby, and Fabian enter. Andrew, assuming that this is the cowardly and dishonest Cesario, strikes Sebastian, whereupon Sebastian (who is more than capable of defending himself) promptly beats Sir Andrew, who surrenders abjectly. Andrew threatens to sue his assailant for battery in the courts. The Clown is perplexed by all this, and goes off to report to Olivia. Sir Toby tries to hold Sebastian, who warns him to let go his hand.

Sir Toby hangs on to his "young soldier" as he calls Sebastian, and tells him to put up his sword. Sebastian indignantly takes out his rapier and sets about Sir Toby; Toby fights back fiercely but not well. At this precise moment the lady Olivia enters, and sees her wretched kinsman about to slay (as she imagines, falsely) her beloved Cesario. The mistaken identities theme is almost complete.

Olivia gives Toby a severe telling-off and sends him away, out of her sight. He leaves, taking the other two with him.

Olivia and Sebastian are left alone, and she makes a fair speech of apology and love to the young man, thinking she is talking to Cesario.

Fabian. A coward, a most devout coward, religious in it.

Sir Andrew. 'Slid, I'll after him again and beat him. 370

Sir Toby. Do; cuff him soundly, but never draw thy sword.

Sir Andrew. An I do not,—   [*Exit.* 400

Fabian. Come, let's see the event.

Sir Toby. I dare lay any money 'twill be nothing yet.

        [*Exeunt.*

ACT FOUR, scene one.

(THE STREET BEFORE OLIVIA'S HOUSE.)

Enter SEBASTIAN *and* Clown.

Clown. Will you make me believe that I am not sent for you?

Sebastian. Go to, go to, thou art a foolish fellow. Let me be clear of thee.

Clown. Well held out, i' faith! No, I do not know you; nor I am not sent to you by my lady, to bid you come speak with her; nor your name is not Master Cesario; nor this is not my nose neither. Nothing that is so is so.

Sebastian. I prithee, vent thy folly somewhere else; 10 Thou know'st not me.

Clown. Vent my folly! he has heard that word of some great man, and now applies it to a fool. Vent my folly! I am afraid this great lubber, the world, will prove a cockney. I prithee now, ungird thy 14 strangeness and tell me what I shall vent to my lady. Shall I vent to her that thou art coming?

Sebastian. I prithee, foolish Greek, depart from me. There's money for thee; if you tarry longer, I shall give worse payment. 19

Clown. By my troth, thou hast an open hand. These wise men that give fools money get themselves a good report—after fourteen years' purchase.

Enter SIR ANDREW, SIR TOBY *and* FABIAN.

Sir Andrew. Now, sir, have I met you again? there's for you.   [*Striking Sebastian.* 23

Sebastian. Why, there's for thee, and there, and there. Are all the people mad?   [*Beating Sir Andrew.*

Sir Toby. Hold, sir, or I'll throw your dagger o'er the house.

Clown. This will I tell my lady straight; I would not be in some of your coats for two pence.   [*Exit.*

Sir Toby. Come on, sir; hold.

Sir Andrew. Nay, let him alone. I'll go another way to work with him: I'll have an action of battery 31 against him, if there be any law in Illyria; though I struck him first, yet it's no matter for that.

Sebastian. Let go thy hand.

Sir Toby. Come, sir, I will not let you go. Come, my young soldier, put up your iron. You are well fleshed; come on.

Sebastian. I will be free from thee. What wouldst

---

370. "'Slid": God's eyelid (a common oath).

400. "Sir Andrew's courage is high": in the absence of the opponent.

Feste has a message to deliver to Cesario for Olivia; he insists on delivering it to Sebastian, much to Sebastian's irritation: He wants to get rid of this foolish fellow!

10. "vent": utter (spoken scornfully).

14. "cockney": those who spoke the dialect and fancy speech of citizens of London.

19. "worse payment": blows, probably.

23. Sir Andrew comes upon, as he thinks, the cowardly Cesario, and strikes him once or twice. Taken by surprise, Sebastian does not at once retaliate; then he beats off Sir Andrew, and wonders if all the people are mad in these parts.

31. "action of battery": lawsuit for assault (yet Sir Andrew began it!)

TWELFTH NIGHT

ACT IV SCENE I

Sebastian finds himself being wooed in the most ardent terms by a beautiful young countess, and he wisely gives up trying to figure it all out. If it is a dream, let me sleep on. Olivia, delighted at the change in her Cesario (as she thinks he is), hastily proposes marriage and is accepted at once. They dash off to look for a priest to perform the ceremony, which, one feels, in the circumstances, will not be long delayed.

ACT IV SCENE II

You will remember that Sir Toby and his other associates had thrown Malvolio, the supposed lunatic, into a dark room after he had appeared before Olivia smiling, dressed in yellow stockings, and cross-gartered. Maria and Feste, the jester, now prepare to carry this "joke" a step further. Feste is disguising himself as a parson, and is going to make a mercy call on the poor mad prisoner. You should note the part played in this play by the various disguises. Disguise might be said to be one of the themes of TWELFTH NIGHT.

Parsons at this time wore black gowns and beards and were frequently referred to by the title Sir. Thus Feste will assume the part of Sir Topas, the curate, who goes to visit Malvolio, the prisoner.

thou now? If thou darest tempt me further, draw thy sword.

Sir Toby. What, what? Nay, then I must have an ounce or two of this malapert blood from you. 40

Enter OLIVIA.

Olivia. Hold, Toby; on thy life I charge thee, hold!

Sir Toby. Madam!

Olivia. Will it be ever thus? Ungracious wretch,
Fit for the mountains and the barbarous caves,
Where manners ne'er were preach'd! out of my sight! 46
Be not offended, dear Cesario.
Rudesby, be gone!

[*Exeunt* SIR TOBY, SIR ANDREW, *and* FABIAN.

I prithee, gentle friend,
Let thy fair wisdom, not thy passion, sway
In this uncivil and unjust extent
Against thy peace. Go with me to my house,
And hear thou there how many fruitless pranks 51
This ruffian hath botch'd up, that thou thereby 52
Mayst smile at this. Thou shalt not choose but go.
Do not deny. Beshrew his soul for me, 54
He started one poor heart of mine in thee. 55

Sebastian. What relish is in this? how runs the stream?
Or I am mad, or else this is a dream.
Let fancy still my sense in Lethe steep; 57
If it be thus to dream, still let me sleep!

Olivia. Nay, come, I prithee; would thou'dst be ruled by me!

Sebastian. Madam, I will.

Olivia. Oh, say so, and so be! [*Exeunt.*

Scene two.

(A ROOM *in* OLIVIA'S HOUSE.)

Enter MARIA *and* Clown.

Maria. Nay, I prithee, put on this gown and this 1
beard; make him believe thou art Sir Topas the 2
curate. Do it quickly; I'll call Sir Toby the whilst. 3
[*Exit.*

Clown. Well, I'll put it on, and I will dissemble my- 4
self in't; and I would I were the first that ever dissembled in such a gown. I am not tall enough to become the function well, nor lean enough to be
thought a good student; but to be said an honest
man and a good housekeeper goes as fairly as to say
a careful man and a great scholar. The competitors 10
enter.

Enter SIR TOBY *and* MARIA.

Sir Toby. Jove bless thee, Master Parson.

Clown. Bonos dies, Sir Toby; for, as the old hermit 13
of Prague, that never saw pen and ink, very wittily
said to a niece of King Gorboduc, "That that is, is";
so I, being Master Parson, am Master Parson; for,
what is "that" but "that," and "is" but "is"?

40. "malapert": impertinent.

46. spoken with angry indignation to Sir Toby; a change of voice and manner are immediately felt when she addresses 'Cesario' (actually, Sebastian).

51. "fruitless pranks": unprofitable practical jokes.

52. "botch'd up": started.

54. "Beshrew": confound.

55. "started": startled.

57. "Lethe": the classical river of unmindfulness.

1. "Nay, etc.": Feste may have been unwilling to put on this disguise.

2. "Sir": usual title for Elizabethan clergymen.
"Topas": the jewel, topaz, was popularly believed to cure madness.

3. "curate": one who has the cure or care of souls.

4. "dissemble": deceive.
There is some satire of the ecclesiastical type in these lines, but it is not bitter or personal.

10. "competitors": Sir Toby and Maria.

13. "Bonos dies": Latin for Good day hermit of Prague and niece of King Gorboduc, figments of Feste's vivid imagination.

TWELFTH NIGHT

ACT IV SCENE II

Sir Toby enters, greeting Master Parson, and Sir Topas (Feste) replies by intoning a lot of gobbledygook commencing with the Latin words for Good Day and ending with a pedantic, nonsensical, and pseudo-metaphysical quibble on the words "that" and "is" (the problem of existence).

Feste imitates the parson well, and now goes in to mislead and deceive Malvolio.

The imprisoned steward is extremely relieved to hear the parson's voice, for he fondly imagines his deliverance from prison is near. This, of course, is not the case. He will remain in his darkness for some time to come.

Although this is a comic scene, it is impossible not to feel a trifle sorry for the self-righteous steward in this mess.

Feste's parody of the language of the church and of ecclesiastical thinking must not be taken too seriously in itself, but must be viewed in terms of the dramatic purpose it is intended to serve, namely additional teasing of Malvolio. Judged by this criterion, it is a very light and successfully humorous scene.

The ultimate absurdity comes when Sir Topas imposes belief in the ancient Pythagorean notion of transmigration of souls (metempsychosis) as a necessary condition to deliverance, or salvation. Did Shakespeare mean to convey that pagan elements had crept into Christian religion by his time? Perhaps. But Malvolio is frustrated and confused by all Sir Topas' nonsense.

Feste creeps out to receive the riotous congratulations of the others.

Feste might have acted the part of the parson before Malvolio without his disguise, for the steward cannot see him. Sir Toby says now go to him and in your natural voice (not the one he assumed for Sir Topas) find out how Malvolio is. He wishes they could release Malvolio and get out of the consequences of the whole business, for he is afraid the lady Olivia will turn him out of her house for this.

They go out, while Feste goes in again to Malvolio, this time singing a merry song, as befits the Clown. Malvolio perks up at the sound of this familiar voice, and pleads for ink, pen, and paper, so that he can write an account of the shameful way he has been treated. He assures Feste that he is not mad, and complains that he has been shut up in this dark room

Sir Toby. To him, Sir Topas.

Clown. What ho, I say! peace in this prison!

Sir Toby. The knave counterfeits well; a good knave.

Malvolio. [*Within.*] Who calls there?

Clown. Sir Topas the curate, who comes to visit Malvolio the lunatic.

Malvolio. Sir Topas, Sir Topas, good Sir Topas, go to my lady.

Clown. Out, hyperbolical fiend! how vexest thou this man! talkest thou nothing but of ladies? 25

Sir Toby. Well said, Master Parson.

Malvolio. Sir Topas, never was man thus wronged. Good Sir Topas, do not think I am mad; they have 29 laid me here in hideous darkness.

Clown. Fie, thou dishonest Satan! I call thee by the most modest terms; for I am one of those gentle ones that will use the devil himself with courtesy. Sayest thou that house is dark?

Malvolio. As hell, Sir Topas.

Clown. Why, it hath bay windows transparent as barricadoes, and the clearstories towards the south 37 north are as lustrous as ebony; and yet complainest thou of obstruction? 39

Malvolio. I am not mad, Sir Topas; I say to you, this house is dark.

Clown. Madman, thou errest. I say, there is no darkness but ignorance, in which thou are more puzzled than the Egyptians in their fog. 44

Malvolio. I say, this house is as dark as ignorance, though ignorance were as dark as hell; and I say, there was never man thus abused. I am no more mad than you are. Make the trial of it in any constant question. 48

Clown. What is the opinion of Pythagoras concerning wild fowl? 49

Malvolio. That the soul of our grandam might haply inhabit a bird.

Clown. What thinkest thou of his opinion?

Malvolio. I think nobly of the soul, and no way approve his opinion. 54

Clown. Fare thee well. Remain thou still in darkness. Thou shalt hold the opinion of Pythagoras ere I will allow of thy wits; and fear to kill a woodcock, lest thou dispossess the soul of thy grandam. Fare thee well.

Malvolio. Sir Topas, Sir Topas!

Sir Toby. My most exquisite Sir Topas!

Clown. Nay, I am for all waters.

Maria. Thou mightst have done this without thy beard and gown: he sees thee not. 64

Sir Toby. To him in thine own voice, and bring me word how thou findest him. I would we were well 66 rid of this knavery. If he may be conveniently delivered, I would he were, for I am now so far in offence with my niece that I cannot pursue with any safety this sport to the upshot. Come by and by to 70 my chamber. [*Exeunt* SIR TOBY *and* MARIA.

Clown. [*Singing.*] Hey, Robin, jolly Robin,
　　　　　Tell me how thy lady does.

Malvolio. Fool!

25. "hyperbolical fiend": diabolical is not good enough for Feste; he suggests an exaggerated devil, that makes Malvolio talk only of women (Olivia).

29. Malvolio is pleading for a change; the physic worked!

37. "barricadoes": barricades (which are not transparent).
"clearstories": clerestories, i.e., small windows above the arches in a church or high up in the hall of a great house.

39. "obstruction": of the light (the place is dark); the word as used here reminds us of Malvolio's triumphant entrance earlier before Olivia when he complained of the cross-gartering obstructing his veins. There is irony in this echo.

44. "Egyptians . . . fog": see Exodus, x, 22-23.

48. "constant question": properly ordered interrogation.

49. "Pythagoras": Greek philosopher and mathematician who taught that after death human souls passed into animals the type of which corresponded to the quality of the life lived before death.

54. As a Puritan, Malvolio could not agree with Pythagoras' pre-Christian teachings about life after death.

64. "he sees thee not": because the place is dark (perhaps this was why Feste was reluctant to put on the beard and gown in the first place).

66. "well rid": Sir Toby wishes they were out of this affair; he senses trouble with Olivia over this 'joke.'

70. "upshot": logical conclusion.

56

TWELFTH NIGHT

ACT IV SCENE II

unjustly, visited by the priest, an ass, at which Feste warns him to watch what he is saying; the minister is here.

Feste then assumes his ecclesiastical voice again, and gives Malvolio another unsuitable admonition.

By changing from one voice to another in rapid succession, Feste gives Malvolio the impression that he has two visitors instead of one. Malvolio, meanwhile, goes on pleading for writing materials.

Finally, persuaded that Malvolio is not insane, he leaves, promising to bring the ink, pen, and writing paper, and singing a merry song that seems to be faintly appropriate: "your need to sustain."

Clown. "My lady is unkind, perdy."

Malvolio. Fool!

Clown. "Alas, why is she so?"

Malvolio. Fool, I say!

Clown. "She loves another"—Who calls, ha?

Malvolio. Good fool, as ever thou wilt deserve well at my hand, help me to a candle, and pen, ink, and paper. As I am a gentleman, I will live to be thankful to thee for't.

Clown. Master Malvolio?

Malvolio. Ay, good fool.

Clown. Alas, sir, how fell you beside your five wits? 84

Malvolio. Fool, there was never man so notoriously abused. I am as well in my wits, fool, as thou art.

Clown. But as well? then you are mad indeed, if you be no better in your wits than a fool.

Malvolio. They have here propertied me; keep me 89 in darkness, send ministers to me, asses, and do all they can to face me out of my wits.

Clown. Advise you what you say; the minister is here. Malvolio, Malvolio, thy wits the heavens re- 93 store! endeavour thyself to sleep, and leave thy vain 94 bibble babble.

Malvolio. Sir Topas!

Clown. Maintain no words with him, good fellow. Who, I, sir? not I, sir. God be wi' you, good Sir Topas. Marry, amen. I will, sir, I will.

Malvolio. Fool, fool, fool, I say!

Clown. Alas, sir, be patient. What say you, sir? I am shent for speaking to you. 101

Malvolio. Good fool, help me to some light and some paper. I tell thee, I am as well in my wits as any man in Illyria.

Clown. Well-a-day that you were, sir!

Malvolio. By this hand, I am. Good fool, some ink, paper, and light; and convey what I will set down to 107 my lady. It shall advantage thee more than ever the 108 bearing of letter did.

Clown. I will help you to't. But tell me true, are you not mad indeed? or do you but counterfeit?

Malvolio. Believe me, I am not; I tell thee true.

Clown. Nay, I'll ne'er believe a madman till I see his brains. I will fetch you light and paper and ink.

Malvolio. Fool, I'll requite it in the highest degree. 115 I prithee, be gone.

Clown. [*Singing.*] I am gone, sir.

> And anon, sir,
> I'll be with you again,
> In a trice,
> Like to the old Vice, 121
> Your need to sustain;
> Who, with dagger of lath,
> In his rage and his wrath,
> Cries, aha! to the devil:
> Like a mad lad,
> Pare thy nails, dad;
> Adieu, goodman devil.

[*Exit.*

84. "fell you . . . five wits": lost your reason.

89. "propertied me": made a tool of.

93. In this speech, Feste alters his position to suit the alterations of his voice, as he plays both the Curate, Sir Topas, and himself.

94. "vain bibble babble": see 1 Timothy, vi, 20; 2 Timothy, ii, 16.

101. "shent": rebuked, reproved, blamed.

107. "convey": carry to my lady.

108. "advantage thee": profit or reward thee.

115. "requite": repay, reimburse.

121. "old Vice": comic character in the mediaeval morality plays.

TWELFTH NIGHT

ACT IV SCENE III

In the lady Olivia's garden, Sebastian experiences the bliss of being loved and great puzzlement as to the basis of his good fortune. He can scarcely believe what is happening to him, and holds up a pearl his lady gave him as tangible proof that he is not still in the world of dreams.

In need of advice, he thinks of Antonio, who might now be able to do him sovereign service. He heard that Antonio did stay at the Elephant, but was unable to find him when he went there to keep their appointment. He has heard that Antonio has been looking for him, without success. Of course, we all know that Antonio was arrested during the Cesario-Sir Andrew duel and its aftermath.

He wonders if he, or Olivia, is mad, but persuades himself that neither is.

While he ponders over these delightful problems, Olivia enters the garden with a priest.

She wishes Sebastian to go with her and the holy man into the little chapel nearby, where they will be wed according to the full rites of the church, so that her jealous and too doubtful soul may live at peace.

This marriage will be kept a close secret. Later, they will have a public ceremony in keeping with her rank.

Sebastian agrees, and they go off arm in arm to the chantry for the private ceremony. An atmosphere of happiness shines throughout this simple scene, and brings the short fourth act to a close.

Scene three.

(OLIVIA'S GARDEN.)

Enter SEBASTIAN.

Sebastian. This is the air; that is the glorious sun;
This pearl she gave me, I do feel't and see't;   2
And though 'tis wonder that enwraps me thus,
Yet 'tis not madness. Where's Antonio, then?
I could not find him at the Elephant;
Yet there he was; and there I found this credit,   6
That he did range the town to seek me out.
His counsel now might do me golden service;   8
For though my soul disputes well with my sense,
That this may be some error, but no madness,
Yet doth this accident and flood of fortune
So far exceed all instance, all discourse,
That I am ready to distrust mine eyes,
And wrangle with my reason, that peruades me
To any other trust but that I am mad,
Or else the lady's mad; yet, if 'twere so,
She could not sway her house, command her
    followers,
Take and give back affairs and their dispatch
With such a smooth, discreet, and stable bearing
As I perceive she does. There's something in't
That is deceivable. But here the lady comes.   21

Enter OLIVIA *and* Priest.
Olivia. Blame not this haste of mine. If you mean
    well,
Now go with me and with this holy man
Into the chantry by. There, before him,   24
And underneath that consecrated roof,
Plight me the full assurance of your faith,   26
That my most jealous and too doubtful soul
May live at peace. He shall conceal it
Whiles you are willing it shall come to note,   29
What time we will our celebration keep
According to my birth. What do you say?   31
Sebastian. I'll follow this good man, and go with
    you;
And, having sworn truth, ever will be true.
Olivia. Then lead the way, good father; and heavens
    so shine,
That they may fairly note this act of mine!   35

[*Exeunt.*

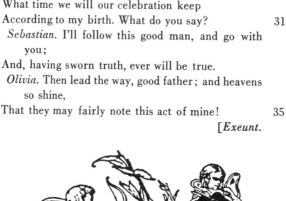

Sebastian is bewildered and blessed with a remarkable opportunity; he cannot believe it, and searches, not unnaturally, for tangible evidence.

2. "This pearl": evidence of Olivia's love.

6. "credit": general view or belief.

8. "counsel": advice, guidance.

21. "deceivable": mistaken.

24. "chantry": private chapel.

26. "Plight me": pledge me.

29. "to note": to public notice.

31. "my birth": Olivia is a countess in her own right now, and deserves a full public wedding ceremony when the time comes.

35. The marriage is Olivia's act, rather than a mutually decided one.

ACT V SCENE I

In this act, which consists of but a single scene, all the other plots, both major and minor, and the theme of mistaken identity with its complications, are unraveled and resolved.

The location is the street, before the countess's house. Feste is carrying Malvolio's letter to Olivia, but Fabian is holding him up with a request to see this letter. Feste does not want to open it for fear of getting into trouble with the countess about it later on, but equally he is in no great hurry to deliver it.

Duke Orsino, Cesario, Curio, and others come in, and the Duke has a few words with the Clown, whom he recognizes. They play with words in a way that Orsino considers excellent. The truth is that anything belonging to Olivia pleases his taste. He, therefore, tips Feste a gold piece.

Feste, having received one gold coin, tries to wheedle another out of the Duke by reference to "double-dealing," and receives a second coin. References in Latin to "tertio" (third) and in English to "third" and "triplex" and "three" follow, to try and get a third coin out of the Duke, but do not succeed. Orsino says go and tell your lady that I am here to speak with her, and if you come back accompanied by her, I may give you some more money.

As Feste goes out, he tells the Duke's generosity to go to sleep until he comes back to awaken it again.

Cesario sees Antonio coming, and tells the Duke that this was the man that rescued her from the duel with Sir Andrew earlier. Antonio is, of course, still under arrest. The Duke remembers Antonio well; when he saw him last, Antonio's face was smeared as black as the god Vulcan in the smoke of battle. He was captain of a pirate vessel and did grave damage to the Duke's fleet.

ACT FIVE, scene one.

(THE STREET BEFORE OLIVIA'S HOUSE.)

Enter Clown *and* FABIAN.

Fabian. Now, as thou lovest me, let me see his letter. 1
Clown. Good master Fabian, grant me another request.
Fabian. Anything.
Clown. Do not desire to see this letter.
Fabian. This is, to give a dog, and in recompense desire my dog again. 6
Enter Duke, VIOLA, CURIO, *and* Lords.
Duke. Belong you to the Lady Olivia, friends?
Clown. Ay, sir, we are some of her trappings. 8
Duke. I know thee well. How dost thou, my good fellow?
Clown. Truly, sir, the better for my foes and the worse for my friends.
Duke. Just the contrary, the better for thy friends.
Clown. No, sir, the worse.
Duke. How can that be?
Clown. Marry, sir, they praise me and make an ass of me; now my foes tell me plainly I am an ass: so that by my foes, sir, I profit in the knowledge of myself, and by my friends I am abused: so that, conclusions to be as kisses, if your four negatives make 19 your two affirmatives, why then, the worse for my friends and the better for my foes.
Duke. Why, this is excellent.
Clown. By my troth, sir, no, though it please you 23 to be one of my friends.
Duke. Thou shalt not be the worse for me. There's gold.
Clown. But that it would be double-dealing, sir, I would you could make it another.
Duke. Oh, you give me ill counsel.
Clown. Put your grace in your pocket, sir, for this 28 once, and let your flesh and blood obey it.
Duke. Well, I will be so much a sinner, to be a double-dealer; there's another.
Clown. Primo, secundo, tertio, is a good play; and 32 the old saying is, the third pays for all. The triplex, 33 sir, is a good tripping measure; or the bells of Saint 34 Bennet, sir, may put you in mind; one, two, three.
Duke. You can fool no more money out of me at this throw. If you will let your lady know I am here to speak with her, and bring her along with you, it may awake my bounty further. 39
Clown. Marry, sir, lullaby to your bounty till I come 40 again. I go, sir, but I would not have you to think that my desire of having is the sin of covetousness; but, as you say, sir, let your bounty take a nap, I will awake it anon. [*Exit.*
Viola. Here comes the man, sir, that did rescue me. 44
Enter ANTONIO *and* Officers.
Duke. That face of his I do remember well;
Yet, when I saw it last it was besmear'd

1. "his": Malvolio's.

6. "again": that is in exchange; so one has given nothing!

8. "trappings": belongings (relate to 'Belong you . . .?' in the previous line).

19-20. "four negatives make your two affirmatives": Feste knows his logic well: he means kissing.

23. "troth": truth.

28. "grace": the title of a Duke, and the source of all charity.

32. "Primo, etc.": a counting game played with dice.

33. "triplex": triple time in music for dancing.

34. "Saint Bennet": probably one of the St. Bennet (Benedict) churches in the city of London.

39. "bounty": generosity.

40. "lullaby to your bounty": may your generosity sleep sweetly until I come again to reawaken it.

44. "the man": Antonio.

TWELFTH NIGHT

ACT V SCENE I

Nevertheless, though an enemy, Antonio was a brave and honorable opponent, and they remember his valor to this day. The first officer says that this is the same Antonio that captured the ship Phoenix and her cargo (freight) from Candy, and the same man that boarded the vessel Tiger on the occasion when Orsino's nephew Titus lost a leg. He was arrested during a street-brawl.

Cesario comes to Antonio's defense; Antonio drew his sword in Cesario's defense, and rescued him (Cesario) from the sword of Sir Andrew Aguecheek.

The Duke asks Antonio to explain how he came to be taken by his enemies. Antonio says that he has never been base or a pirate, though he does admit to having been Orsino's enemy in the past, with good reason. He blames his fate on witchcraft. He rescued that ungrateful boy there (Cesario) from the waves during and after the shipwreck and did him notable service, even lending him his purse.

This fellow showed his ungratefulness by denying acquaintance with Antonio, refusing to recognize him, and refusing to give back the purse. He is indignant over the ungratefulness of this repudiation.

Cesario asks how is this possible? She has never seen this man before, except when he delivered her from the sword of Sir Andrew.

Orsino asks Antonio when this young man came to town, and Antonio says, "to-day, my lord," and for three months before that they kept company day and night.

There is an obvious inconsistency here, and we know that Antonio is mistaking Viola for Sebastian; the truth does not come out yet, however.

The countess Olivia makes a grand entrance with her attendants, looking radiantly happy. For the Duke, heaven now walks on earth; and he does not hesitate to dismiss Antonio as a madman.

Olivia asks Orsino grandly what he wants, apart from what he cannot have; she also accuses Cesario of having broken faith with her.

Cesario has no idea what Olivia is talking about. Her startled exclamation, "Madam!" indicates this. Olivia addresses Cesario before the Duke, and this embarrasses Cesario, who tells Olivia his duty does not let him speak before his lord.

As black as Vulcan in the smoke of war. 47
A bawbling vessel was he captain of, 48
For shallow draught and bulk unprizable, 49
With which such scathful grapple did he make 50
With the most noble bottom of our fleet, 51
That very envy and the tongue of loss 52
Cried fame and honour on him. What's the matter?
First Officer. Orsino, this is that Antonio
That took the Phoenix and her fraught from Candy; 55
And this is he that did the Tiger board,
When your young nephew Titus lost his leg.
Here in the streets, desperate of shame and state,
In private brabble did we apprehend him. 59
Viola. He did me kindness, sir, drew on my side; 60
But in conclusion put strange speech upon me, 61
I know not what 'twas but distraction. 62
Duke. Notable pirate! thou salt-water thief!
What foolish boldness brought thee to their mercies,
Whom thou, in terms so bloody and so dear,
Hast made thine enemies?
Antonio. Orsino, noble sir,
Be pleased that I shake off these names you give me.
Antonio never yet was thief or pirate,
Though I confess, on base and ground enough,
Orsino's enemy. A witchcraft drew me hither.
That most ingrateful boy there by your side, 71
From the rude sea's enraged and foamy mouth 72
Did I redeem; a wreck past hope he was.
His life I gave him and did thereto add
My love, without retention or restraint, 75
All his in dedication; for his sake
Did I expose myself, pure for his love,
Into the danger of this adverse town; 78
Drew to defend him when he was beset: 79
Where being apprehended, his false cunning,
Not meaning to partake with me in danger,
Taught him to face me out of his acquaintance, 82
And grew a twenty years removed thing
While one could wink; denied me mine own purse,
Which I had recommended to his use 85
Not half an hour before.
Viola. How can this be?
Duke. When came he to this town?
Antonio. To-day, my lord; and for three months before,
No interim, not a minute's vacancy,
Both day and night did we keep company. 90
Enter OLIVIA *and* Attendants.
Duke. Here comes the countess; now heaven walks on earth.
But for thee, fellow,—fellow, thy words are madness.
Three months this youth hath tended upon me;
But more of that anon. Take him aside. 93
Olivia. What would my lord, but that he may not have,
Wherein Olivia may seem serviceable?
Cesario, you do not keep promise with me.
Viola. Madam! 98
Duke. Gracious Olivia,—

47. "Vulcan": Roman god of fire and metal-work.

48. "bawbling": small.

49. "unprizable": worthless.

50. "scathful grapple": damaging attack.

51. "bottom of our fleet": vessel.

52. "That, etc.": that even those who had suffered loss envied him his success and honored him for his famous achievement.

55. 'fraught': freight, cargo.
"Candy": ancient capital of Crete.

59. "apprehend": seize or arrest.

60. "drew": drew his sword.

61. "strange speech": unintelligible words.

62. "distraction": madness.

71. "ingrateful": ungrateful (Antonio thinks the boy is Sebastian, whereas we know it is Viola in disguise still).

72. "rude": rough.
"mouth": personification of the sea.

75. "retention": withholding or holding back.

78. "adverse": hostile.

79. "beset": attacked.

82. "face me out of his acquaintance": brazenly deny ever having known me.

85. "recommended to his use": urged upon him.

90. Before the contradiction between Antonio's evidence and the Duke's own knowledge can be brought out, the lady Olivia and her attendants make a grand entrance which distracts everybody from the business in hand.

93. Orsino has Antonio taken aside.

98. Olivia's accusation takes Viola completely by surprise!

TWELFTH NIGHT

ACT V SCENE 1

Olivia makes it plain she does not want to hear "aught to the old tune" from the Duke.

The Duke is thunder-struck. He calls her an uncivil lady and threatens to kill what he loves. He knows that she loves Cesario, his minion, and tells her that he is going to take him away with him. "Come, boy, with me," he says. Cesario goes willingly. Olivia is appalled; is her new husband about to walk out on her?

Where are you going? she asks Cesario. After him I love more than I love myself, replies Cesario. Olivia feels utterly betrayed and rejected.

She calls forth the holy father, the priest who recently married her to Cesario (as she thought he was).

The priest comes in a few seconds later, and attests to the fact of the marriage between these two having recently taken place. Olivia thinks it is the baseness of Cesario's fear (as the Duke's minion) that made him deny the marriage, and she tries to reinforce his confidence.

Olivia. What do you say, Cesario? Good my lord,—
Viola. My lord would speak; my duty hushes me.   101
Olivia. If it be aught to the old tune, my lord,
It is as fat and fulsome to mine ear
As howling after music.
Duke.   Still so cruel?
Olivia. Still so constant, lord.
Duke. What, to perverseness? you uncivil lady,
To whose ingrate and unauspicious altars   107
My soul the faithfull'st offerings hath breathed out
That e'er devotion tender'd! What shall I do?
Olivia. Even what it please my lord, that shall become him.
Duke. Why should I not, had I the heart to do it,
Like to the Egyptian thief at point of death,   112
Kill what I love?—a savage jealousy
That sometimes savours nobly. But hear me this:
Since you to non-regardance cast my faith,
And that I partly know the instrument
That screws me from my true place in your favour,
Live you the marble-breasted tyrant still;
But this your minion, whom I know you love,   119
And whom, by heaven I swear, I tender dearly,
Him will I tear out of that cruel eye,
Where he sits crowned in his master's spite.
Come, boy, with me; my thoughts are ripe in mischief.
I'll sacrifice the lamb that I do love,
To spite a raven's heart within a dove.
Viola. And I, most jocund, apt, and willingly,   126
To do you rest, a thousand deaths would die.   127
Olivia. Where goes Cesario?
Viola.   After him I love
More than I love these eyes, more than my life,
More, by all mores, than e'er I shall love wife.
If I do feign, you witnesses above   131
Punish my life for tainting of my love!   132
Olivia. Ay me, detested! how am I beguiled!   133
Viola. Who does beguile you? who does do you wrong?
Olivia. Hast thou forgot thyself? is it so long?
Call forth the holy father.
Duke.   Come, away!
Olivia. Whither, my lord? Cesario, husband, stay.
Duke. Husband!
Olivia.   Ay, husband: can he that deny?
Duke. Her husband, sirrah!
Viola.   No, my lord, not I.
Olivia. Alas, it is the baseness of thy fear
That makes thee strangle thy propriety.   141
Fear not, Cesario; take thy fortunes up;
Be that thou know'st thou art, and then thou art
As great as that thou fear'st.
                Enter Priest.
Oh, welcome, father!
Father, I charge thee, by thy reverence,
Here to unfold, though lately we intended
To keep in darkness what occasion now
Reveals before 'tis ripe, what thou dost know
Hath newly pass'd between this youth and me.

101. Viola's attitude takes Olivia by surprise; they are really at cross-purposes.

107. "ingrate": ungrateful.
"inauspicious altars": unhappy places of worship.

112. "Egyptian thief": reference to Thyamis, a character in a Greek novel, who tried to kill his lover Chariclea to prevent her from falling into the hands of their enemies, but who killed the wrong person; Chariclea escaped. Translated into English in 1569. (Theagenes)

119. "minion": darling; also servant.

126. "jocund": merrily.

127. "To do you rest": to give you peace of mind.

131. "feign": pretend.

132. "tainting": spoiling.

133. "beguiled": betrayed and tricked.

141. It is your fear (as an employee of the Duke's) that makes you deny the truth.

61

TWELFTH NIGHT

ACT V SCENE I

The priest reveals to the astonished group that he performed the marriage ceremony uniting the countess and Cesario not two hours ago that very day.

Orsino is convinced. He calls Cesario a "dissembling cub" and dismisses him. He says, "take her; but direct thy feet/Where thou and I henceforth may never meet."
Poor Cesario tries to protest, but Olivia interrupts him.

Suddenly Sir Andrew Aguecheek enters, calling loudly for a surgeon. Sir Toby also needs one. They have been wounded by the count's gentleman, one Cesario. Andrew has had his head broken across, and Toby has a bloody coxcomb too.

Sir Andrew's description of their assailant as a very devil scarcely fits the Duke's gentleman, Cesario. Yet both Andrew and Toby, who shortly after enters holding his bleeding head and in a drunken condition, bear evidence of the attack. Who is lying?

Olivia asks who has made this havoc with them, but nobody replies, and the crestfallen crew go out holding one another up.

Priest. A contract of eternal bond of love, 150
Confirm'd by mutual joinder of your hands, 151
Attested by the holy close of lips, 152
Strengthen'd by interchangement of your rings;
And all the ceremony of this compact 154
Seal'd in my function, by my testimony:
Since when, my watch hath told me, toward my
    grave
I have trevell'd but two hours.
Duke. O thou dissembling cub! what wilt thou be 158
When time hath sow'd a grizzle on thy case? 159
Or will not else thy craft so quickly grow,
That thine own trip shall be thine overthrow?
Farewell, and take her; but direct thy feet
Where thou and I henceforth may never meet.
Viola. My lord, I do protest—
Olivia.   Oh, do not swear!
Hold little faith, though thou hast too much fear.

Enter SIR ANDREW.

Sir Andrew. For the love of God, a surgeon! Send one presently to Sir Toby.
Olivia. What's the matter?
Sir Andrew. He has broke my head across and has given Sir Toby a bloody coxcomb too. For the love 170 of God, your help! I had rather than forty pound I were at home.
Olivia. Who has done this, Sir Andrew?
Sir Andrew. The count's gentleman, one Cesario. We took him for a coward, but he's the very devil incardinate. 174
Duke. My gentleman, Cesario?
Sir Andrew. 'Od's lifelings! Here he is! You broke 176 my head for nothing; and that that I did, I was set 177 on to do't by Sir Toby. 178
Viola. Why do you speak to me? I never hurt you:
You drew your sword upon me without cause;
But I bespake you fair, and hurt you not.
Sir Andrew. If a bloody coxcomb be a hurt, you have hurt me: I think you set nothing by a bloody coxcomb. [*Enter* SIR TOBY *and* Clown.] Here comes Sir Toby halting; you shall hear more: but if he had 184 not been in drink, he would have tickled you other- 185 gates than he did.
Duke. How now, gentleman! how is't with you?
Sir Toby. That's all one; has hurt me, and there's the end on't. Sot, didst see Dick surgeon, sot? 189
Clown. Oh, he's drunk, Sir Toby, an hour agone; his eyes were set at eight i' the morning. 191
Sir Toby. Then he's a rogue, and a passy measures 192 pavin. I hate a drunken rogue.
Olivia. Away with him! Who hath made this havoc 194 with them?
Sir Andrew. I'll help you, Sir Toby, because we'll be dressed together.
Sir Toby. Will you help? an ass-head and a coxcomb 198 and a knave, a thin-faced knave, a gull!
Olivia. Get him to bed, and let his hurt be looked to.
        [*Exeunt* Clown, FABIAN, SIR TOBY,
             and SIR ANDREW.

150. "contract": marriage-agreement.

151. "mutual joinder": reciprocal joining.

152. "Attested": witnessed by.
"holy close of lips": kissing.

154. "ceremony of this compact": ritual of the matrimonial agreement.
The language of the priest is both legal and theological, since he has performed a civil and a religious ceremony within the last two hours.

158. Orsino thinks Cesario has been dissembling, or playing a double game, all this time. So in another sense, she has.
"dissembling cub": deceiving youth.

159. "sow'd a grizzle on thy case": grown a beard on your face.

170. "coxcomb": ludicrous name for the head.

174. "incardinate": incarnate (in the flesh).

176. "'Od's lifelings": God's lifelings (a common Elizabethan oath).

177-8. "set on to do't": put up to it (by).

184. "halting": limping.

185. "othergates": otherwise (than).

189. "sot": fool.

191. "set": glazed or glassy with drink.

192. "passy measures pavin": Italian passermezzo pavana, a slow and stately dance.

194. "havoc": devastation.

198. "Will you help, etc": Sir Toby's scorn for Sir Andrew here falls into downright irritation and contempt.

TWELFTH NIGHT

ACT V SCENE I

The key to the solution of all these puzzles now enters in the person of Sebastian. The most striking thing about him is his close physical resemblance to Cesario; dressed as men, it is almost impossible to distinguish between them except by the colors of their clothes.

Sebastian addresses Olivia; he apologizes for having hurt her relative, but would have done the same even to his own brother had he been treated so. He reminds her of the vows they exchanged such a short while ago, and calls her his sweet one.

Orsino is amazed: one face, one voice, one habit, and two persons! Sebastian greets Antonio as his dear friend, and says he has been undergoing torture during the hours they have spent apart. Antonio asks incredulously if this is really Sebastian. He asks, how has he made division of himself? An apple cut in two is not more alike. Olivia is relieved and pleased at finding that her husband has not deserted her after all.

Sebastian looks at Cesario and asks if that is a reflection of himself. He never had a brother; but he had a sister once, but she was drowned at sea in the shipwreck. Sebastian asks him if he is related to himself.

Cesario says her home is in Messaline. Her father was called Sebastian; so was her brother, but he, alas, was drowned at sea.

Sebastian sees all the pieces but one falling into place; if Cesario were a woman, he would acknowledge her, but this does not seem to be the case. Appearances are deceiving, yet before relinquishing her masculine role Viola further corroborates Sebastian's identity. She mentions her father's distinguishing marks, and receives corroboration from Sebastian.

Viola then reveals the fact that she is a maiden and Sebastian's sister. To prove which she plans to take them to a captain in the town who knew of her disguise and is keeping her women's clothes for her.

Sebastian explains to Olivia that she has been mistaken, else would she have been married to a girl! But it was a natural mistake, and she is now betrothed to a man (who is also virginal).

Enter SEBASTIAN.

Sebastian. I am sorry, madam, I have hurt your kinsman;
But, had it been the brother of my blood, 202
I must have done no less with wit and safety.
You throw a strange regard upon me, and by that
I do perceive it hath offended you.
Pardon me, sweet one, even for the vows
We made each other but so late ago.
Duke. One face, one voice, one habit, and two persons,
A natural perspective, that is, and is not! 209
Sebastian. Antonio, O my dear Antonio!
How have the hours rack'd and tortured me 211
Since I have lost thee!
Antonio. Sebastian are you?
Sebastian. Fear'st thou that, Antonio?
Antonio. How have you made division of yourself?
An apple, cleft in two, is not more twin
Than these two creatures. Which is Sebastian?
Olivia. Most wonderful!
Sebastian. Do I stand there? I never had a brother;
Nor can there be that deity in my nature, 219
Of here and everywhere. I had a sister, 220
Whom the blind waves and surges have devour'd.
Of charity, what kin are you to me?
What countryman? what name? what parentage?
Viola. Of Messaline. Sebastion was my father;
Such a Sebastian was my brother too,
So went he suited to his watery tomb. 226
If spirits can assume both form and suit,
You come to fright us.
Sebastian. A spirit I am indeed;
But am in that dimension grossly clad
Which from the womb I did participate.
Were you a woman, as the rest goes even,
I should my tears let fall upon your cheek,
And say, "Thrice-welcome, drowned Viola!"
Viola. My father had a mole upon his brow. 234
Sebastian. And so had mine.
Viola. And died that day when Viola from her birth
Had number'd thirteen years.
Sebastian. Oh, that record is lively in my soul!
He finished indeed his mortal act
That day that made my sister thirteen years.
Viola. If nothing lets to make us happy both
But this my masculine usurp'd attire, 242
Do not embrace me till each circumstance
Of place, time, fortune, do cohere and jump
That I am Viola: which to confirm,
I'll bring you a captain in this town,
Where lie my maiden weeds; by whose gentle help 247
I was preserved to serve this noble count.
All the occurrence of my fortune since
Hath been between this lady and this lord.
Sebastian. [*To Olivia.*] So comes it, lady, you have 251
been mistook;
But nature to her bias drew in that. 253
You would have been contracted to a maid;
Nor are you therein, by my life, deceived;

202. The arrival of Sebastian (the double of Cesario) throws everybody into a state of amazement.

209. "natural perspective": an optical device common in Elizabethan times was the glass which showed one image when viewed from the front, and another image when viewed from an angle.

211. "rack'd": reference to the rack, an instrument of torture.

219-20. "deity in my nature/Of here and everywhere": reference to the idea (expressed clearly in the English Book of Common Prayer) that it is against the nature of things for anything to be in more than one place at the same time.

226. "suited": dressed.

234. "mole": congenital spot on the skin, usually brown; a birth-mark, evidence of identification.

242. Here Viola reveals the fact that she is a girl disguised as a man.

247. "maiden weeds": girl's clothes.

251. "mistook": archaic form for mistaken.

253. "But nature to her bias": nature led you truly in this (else you would have been married to a girl).

63

TWELFTH NIGHT

ACT V SCENE I

With typical selfishness, the Duke thinks he too will have a share in this most happy shipwreck. He says to Viola that she has told him a thousand times he (Cesario) would never love a woman like to him. Viola confirms this with additions. The Duke says "give me thy hand" (probably a proposal of marriage) and asks to see her in her women's clothes.

The captain who is keeping her clothes is being held for something to do with Malvolio. Olivia sends for Malvolio, but then remembers the steward was much distracted in his wits.

At this moment Feste enters (he has obviously been waiting until the time is ripe) with the letter from Malvolio, who is apparently still in prison.

Feste jests about having to deliver the madman's letter, and, when Olivia tells him to read it aloud, does so in an affected voice to make everybody laugh. Olivia is annoyed at this and soon hands the letter to Fabian to read properly.

Olivia asks if Malvolio really wrote this letter, and the Duke says it savors not much of madness.

Malvolio's sanity having been established, Olivia sends Fabian to bring the steward to the house.

You are betroth'd both to a maid and man.

Duke. Be not amazed; right noble is his blood.
If this be so, as yet the glass seems true,
I shall have share in his most happy wreck.   258
[*To Viola.*] Boy, thou hast said to me a thousand
  times
Thou never shouldst love woman like to me.

Viola. And all those sayings will I over-swear;
And all those swearings keep as true in soul
As doth that orbed continent the fire   263
That severs day from night.

Duke.   Give me thy hand;
And let me see thee in thy woman's weeds.

Viola. The captain that did bring me first on shore
Hath my maid's garments. He upon some action
Is now in durance, at Malvolio's suit,   268
A gentleman, and follower of my lady's.

Olivia. He shall enlarge him. Fetch Malvolio hither;
And yet, alas, now I remember me,
They say, poor gentleman, he's much distract.

          Re-enter Clown *with a letter, and* FABIAN.

A most extracting frenzy of mine own
From my remembrance clearly banish'd his.
How does he, sirrah?

Clown. Truly, madam, he holds Beelzebub at the   276
stave's end as well as a man in his case may do: has
here writ a letter to you; I should have given 't to you
to-day morning, but as a madman's epistles are no   278
gospels, so it skills not much when they are de-   279
livered.

Olivia. Open't, and read it.

Clown. Look then to be well edified when the fool   282
delivers the madman. [*Reads*] "By the Lord,   283
madam,"—

Olivia. How now! art thou mad?

Clown. No, madam, I do but read madness; an
your ladyship will have it as it ought to be, you
must allow Vox.   288

Olivia. Prithee, read i' thy right wits.

Clown. So I do, madonna; but to read his right
wits is to read thus: therefore perpend, my princess,   290
and give ear.

Olivia. Read it you, sirrah.   [*To Fabian.*]   291

Fabian. [*Reads*] "By the Lord, madam, you wrong
me, and the world shall know it. Though you have
put me into darkness and given your drunken cousin   294
rule over me, yet have I the benefit of my senses as
well as your ladyship. I have your own letter that
induced me to the semblance I put on; with the   297
which I doubt not but to do myself much right, or
you much shame. Think of me as you please. I leave
my duty a little unthought of, and speak out of my
injury."   300
          "THE MADLY-USED MALVOLIO."

Olivia. Did he write this?

Clown. Ay, madam.

Duke. This savours not much of distraction.

Olivia. See him deliver'd, Fabian; bring him   305
  hither.   [*Exit* FABIAN.

258. Orsino forgets about his previous passion for Olivia, and sets his sights on Viola now that she is attainable.

263. "orbed continent the fire": the stars.

268. "in durance": waiting trial in prison. "suit": instigation.

276. "Beelzebub": Satan.

278-9. "epistles . . . gospels": letters . . . good news.

282-3. "fool delivers the madman": play on words (to further delay Malvolio's now inevitable deliverance from the dark room?) A play on the two meanings as in delivering a speech and delivering somebody from prison.

288. "Vox": Latin for voice. The Clown uses a solemn and ridiculous voice to make fun of Malvolio.

290. "perpend": listen carefully.

291. Olivia seizes the letter from Feste and hands it to Fabian.

294. "drunken cousin": Sir Toby Belch.

297. "induced me": led me. "semblance": the costume as recommended by the letter.

300. "THE MADLY-USED MALVOLIO": suggests that though he has been treated as though he were mad, the truth is otherwise.

305. Have Malvolio released and brought here.

TWELFTH NIGHT

ACT V SCENE I

Olivia then suggests that Orsino and Sebastian shall each be married, he to Viola (ex-Cesario), she publicly to Sebastian, on the same day, at the same hour, in a double wedding to be held at the countess's house, at her expense.

To this, he joyfully agrees. He then dismisses Cesario, and reappoints Viola as her master's mistress.

Olivia and Viola thus become sisters-in-law.

Fabian now enters with Malvolio. The steward is glowering with rage and quivering with righteous indignation. He accuses Olivia of having done him grievous wrong. He hands her the original letter and asks her to deny that the handwriting in it is her own. She glances at it and tells him that it is not hers though there is a close resemblance to her own style of writing.

Olivia says it is unquestionably Maria's handwriting. It was Maria who first told her Malvolio was mad. Yet he shall be both the plaintiff and judge of his own case later on.

Fabian asks permission to speak and confesses it was himself and Sir Toby who made up this trick against Malvolio.

Maria wrote the letter to oblige Sir Toby. As a reward, he has since married her. The sportful malice they played on Malvolio was not entirely undeserved by him. There have been faults on both sides.

My lord, so please you, these things further thought on,
To think me as well a sister as a wife,
One day shall crown the alliance on't, so please you, 308
Here at my house and at my proper cost.
Duke. Madam, I am most apt to embrace your offer.
[*To Viola.*] Your master quits you; and for your service done him,
So much against the mettle of your sex,
So far beneath your soft and tender breeding,
And since you call'd me master for so long,
Here is my hand. You shall from this time be
Your master's mistress. 316
Olivia. A sister! you are she.

Re-enter FABIAN *with* MALVOLIO.

Duke. Is this the madman?
Olivia. Ay, my lord, the same.
How now, Malvolio?
Malvolio. Madam, you have done me wrong,
Notorious wrong.
Olivia. Have I, Malvolio? no.
Malvolio. Lady, you have. Pray you, peruse that 320
letter.
You must not now deny it is your hand.
Write from it, if you can, in hand or phrase;
Or say 'tis not your seal, not your invention.
You can say none of this; well, grant it then,
And tell me, in the modesty of honour,
Why you have given me such clear lights of favour,
Bade me come smiling and cross-garter'd to you,
To put on yellow stockings and to frown
Upon Sir Toby and the lighter people;
And, acting this in an obedient hope,
Why have you suffer'd me to be imprison'd,
Kept in a dark house, visited by the priest,
And made the most notorious geck and gull
That e'er invention play'd on? tell me why.
Olivia. Alas, Malvolio, this is not my writing,
Though, I confess, much like the character;
But out of question 'tis Maria's hand.
And now I do bethink me, it was she
First told me thou wast mad; then camest in smiling,
And in such forms which here were presupposed
Upon thee in the letter. Prithee, be content.
This practice hath most shrewdly pass'd upon thee;
But when we know the grounds and authors of it,
Thou shalt be both the plaintiff and the judge
Of thine own cause.
Fabian. Good madam, hear me speak.
And let no quarrel nor no brawl to come
Taint the condition of this present hour,
Which I have wonder'd at. In hope it shall not,
Most freely I confess, myself and Toby 349
Set this device against Malvolio here,
Upon some stubborn and uncourteous parts
We had conceived against him. Maria writ
The letter at Sir Toby's great importance;
In recompense whereof he hath married her. 354
How with a sportful malice it was follow'd, 355

308. "One day shall crown the alliance on't": the double marriage shall take place at the same time, at Olivia's house, and at her expense.

316. "master's mistress": an irresistible play on masculine-feminine words.

320. Malvolio is outraged; there is no humor, no charity, no forgiveness in him; and at this point he frustrates any sympathy we might otherwise have been tempted to feel for him. Malvolio neatly sums up the history of his misfortunes, which provides a resume of the play from his point of view.

349. Fabian confesses that he and Toby played the trick on Malvolio, and that Maria wrote the letter at Sir Toby's urgent request. Who is Fabian protecting?

354. Sir Toby has married Maria as a reward for getting Malvolio into trouble.

355. "sportful malice": in this trick there is more matter for laughter than revenge, though all Malvolio can see is revenge.

TWELFTH NIGHT

ACT V SCENE I

Feste then delivers some of the key phrases from the original letter, and Malvolio alternatively squirms and scowls. He goes out in a rage, shaking his fist and swearing to be revenged on the whole lot of them.

Olivia agrees that Malvolio has been "most notoriously abused" and the Duke sends after him, entreating him to "a peace." Malvolio has not told them yet about the captain mentioned by Viola as having been summoned at Malvolio's request.

In lines of stately blank verse, Orsino ends the courtly part of the play, as they all go out with the exception of the Clown.

Feste is left upon the stage as the lights dim, and sings one of the most philosophical clown's songs in the whole of Shakesperean drama.

It tells of the development of man, showing the various stages, and puts all the serious matters of the life of man into the dramatic context of this comedy, whose purpose is simply to entertain us "every day."

May rather pluck on laughter than revenge,
If that the injuries be justly weigh'd
That have on both sides pass'd.
Olivia. Alas, poor fool, how have they baffled thee!
Clown. Why, "some are born great, some achieve greatness, and some have greatness thrown upon them." I was one, sir, in this interlude, one Sir Topas, sir; but that's all one. "By the Lord, fool, I am not mad." But do you remember? "Madam, why laugh you at such a barren rascal? an you smile not, he's gagged." and thus the whirligig of Time brings in his revenges.
Malvolio. I'll be revenged on the whole pack of you.
　　　　　　　　　　　　　　　　　　　[*Exit.*

Olivia. He hath been most notoriously abused.
Duke. Pursue him, and entreat him to a peace.
He hath not told us of the captain yet.　　370
When that is known and golden time convents,
A solemn combination shall be made
Of our dear souls. Meantime, sweet sister,
We will not part from hence. Cesario, come;
For so you shall be, while you are a man;
But when in other habits you are seen,
Orsino's mistress and his fancy queen.
　　　　　　　　　　　　　[*Exeunt all, but* Clown.

Clown. [*Sings.*]
　　When that I was and a little tiny boy,　378
　　　　With hey, ho, the wind and the rain,
　　A foolish thing was but a toy,
　　　　For the rain it raineth every day.

　　But when I came to man's estate,　382
　　　　With hey, ho, the wind and the rain,
　　'Gainst knaves and thieves men shut their gate,
　　　　For the rain it raineth every day.

But when I came, alas! to wive,　386
　　　　With hey, ho, the wind and the rain,
　　By swaggering could I never thrive,
　　　　For the rain it raineth every day.

　　But when I came unto my beds,　390
　　　　With hey, ho, the wind and the rain,
　　With tosspots still had drunken heads,
　　　　For the rain it raineth every day.

　　A great while ago the world begun,　394
　　　　With hey, ho, the wind and the rain,
　　But that's all one, our play is done,
　　　　And we'll strive to please you every day.
　　　　　　　　　　　　　　　　　　　　[*Exit.*

370. The only matter outstanding is that of the captain.
The play ends on a note of harmony and peace. Music might gently play at the close, to introduce the song of Feste the jester.

378. The boy. (Stage 1)

382. The grown men. (Stage 2)

386. Married state. (Stage 3)

390. Senility. (Stage 4)

394. The end. (Stage 5)

Bibliography

EDITIONS

A New Variorum Edition of Shakespeare, ed. Horace H. Furness. New York: J. B. Lippincott, 1871-1919. (Reprints by The American Scholar and Dover Publications.) Each play is dealt with in a separate volume of monumental scholarship.

The Yale Shakespeare, ed. Helge Kökeritz and Charles T. Prouty. New Haven: Yale University Press, 1955——. A multi-volume edition founded on modern scholarship.

COMMENTARY AND CRITICISM

Bentley, G. E. *Shakespeare ₂nd His Theatre.* Lincoln: University of Nebraska Press, 1964 (paperback). Illuminating discussion of the actual conditions under which, and for which, Shakespeare wrote.

Bradley, A. C. *Shakespearean Tragedy: Lectures on Hamlet, Othello, King Lear, Macbeth.* New York: Macmillan, 1904. (Paperback ed.; New York: Meridian Books, 1955.) A classic examination of the great tragedies.

Chambers, Edmund K. *William Shakespeare: A Study of Facts and Problems,* 2 vols. Oxford: Clarendon Press, 1930. Indispensable source for bibliographical and historical information.

Chute, Marchette. *Shakespeare of London.* New York: E. P. Dutton, 1949. A vivid account of Shakespeare's career in the dynamic Elizabethan metropolis.

Granville-Barker, Harley. *Prefaces to Shakespeare.* London: Sidgwick & Jackson, 1927-47. (2 vols.; Princeton: Princeton University Press, 1947.) Stimulating studies of ten plays by a scholarly man of the theater.

Harbage, Alfred. *Shakespeare's Audience.* New York: Columbia University Press, 1941. Revealing approach to Shakespeare as a practical man of the theater.

Knight, Wilson. *The Wheel of Fire.* London: Oxford University Press, 1930. Stresses the power of intuition to capture the total poetic experience of Shakespeare's work.

Spurgeon, Caroline. *Shakespeare's Imagery and What It Tells Us.* Cambridge: Cambridge University Press, 1935. A psychological study of the playwright's imagery as a means to understanding the man himself.